A HISTORY OF THE JEWISH PEOPLE
AND THEIR PROMISED LAND

A HISTORY OF

THE JEWISH PEOPLE AND THEIR PROMISED LAND

EVA GOLDMANN · ZEEV GOLDMANN

with 79 black-and-white illustrations

12 maps

and 70 colour plates by

HED WIMMER

THAMES AND HUDSON · LONDON

Translated from the German
das Land, das Ich dir zeigen werde
Israel und seine Jahrtausende
by Betty Ross

Layout: Emil M. Bührer

CONTENTS

THE PEOPLE OF RETURN

Jew with Torah, Gouache by Marc Chagall (1966).

Of all the civilized nations of our time, probably no other has survived, as Israel has done, so long and stormy a past to emerge into a living present.

A family of shepherds in the second millennium before the Christian era, a sovereign kingdom in the first, the source of the ideals and civilization of the Christian world at the time of transition, dispersed over the face of the earth soon after, they have now, in the twentieth century, returned to the place which their fathers first called their own.

When on 14 May 1948 Israel proclaimed herself an independent state, the deepest wound from which her people had ever suffered was still fresh and smarting. Six hundred thousand members of a decimated people occupied a small sector of their erstwhile kingdom, while thousands waited outside as she opened her gates.

But this was not the first time that the children of Israel had returned home to the country with which they had ties going back to their earliest history. Three times they had returned from strange lands, sometimes but not always driven by necessity. The first time, led by Moses from Egypt where they had been in bondage; the second, from Babylon where many of them had achieved wealth and status; and lastly in our own time, when they found that a people without a country is a defenceless people.

THE LEGACY OF ISRAEL

Ethical monotheism began with Israel, whose covenant with God had turned her from a tribe into a nation. It came from the east and gained the west through Christianity, to return again with Islam to its place of origin—the east. How the tribe became a nation and their God the Lord of the earth, can be found in the books of the Old Testament where the history of the People of Israel is told from the beginning.

The Old Testament is not a unified work. This is clear from the many, sometimes literal, repetitions, and the varying accounts of the same event, which also give rise to doubts about its historical reliability. Bible scholars of the nineteenth century tended to regard it as a significant literary work, and their research into its formal and stylistic variations led them to the conclusion that the Old Testament had been written at different times—often centuries after the event—by different authors. They assumed that individual accounts, while they were based on oral tradition, were largely coloured by the spirit of the time in which they were set down. But archaeological discoveries in Palestine and the Near East provided surprising confirmation of the Old Testament as an historical source. Mesopotamian excavations have produced an abundance of documents from the second millennium B.C., many of which go to prove the authentic nature of the Biblical stories. They point to the world of the ancient Middle East where the People of Israel originated.

The family of Abraham was and remained part of this eastern world, but was lifted by the intuition and genius of its progenitor into another spiritual plane. Abraham renounced the worship of the many deities of his ancestors. God, the one and only God, revealed himself to him. And this one God demanded perfection.

In Asia Minor around the fifteenth century B.C. there existed a form of religion which contained within itself the seeds of higher development. The faith of the Hurrians and Hittites, who lived in close community, knew a god of justice and righteousness and was altogether ethical in intent. But its strength was sapped through a tolerance of new deities so excessive that these eventually attained the impressive figure of the 'thousand gods of Hattusas'.

Pharaoh Amenhotep IV (1378–1362 B.C.), who vigorously upheld the sole authority of his god Aton, came very close to a monotheistic concept of God, but one which in no way impinged on the deification of the Pharaoh and which had no ethical content.

At about the same time in Babylon there arose a pantheistic god of a most unusual kind: each member of the god Ninurta symbolized a deity of the Mesopotamian Olympus. This curious concept left the principle unchanged, for the 'one god' Ninurta continued in essence to represent the forces of nature as they appear in polytheist religions.

But in the case of Abraham, something entirely new began. This man's God could say to him: 'Walk before me and be thou perfect', an admonition not specific as yet

O worship the Lord
in the beauty of holiness:
fear before him, all the earth.
Say among the heathen
that the Lord reigneth:
the world also
shall be established
that it shall not be moved:
he shall judge
the people righteously.
Let the heavens rejoice,
and let the earth be glad:
let the sea roar, and
the fulness thereof.
Let the field be joyful,
and all that is therein:
then shall all the trees
of the wood rejoice
before the Lord:
for he cometh,
for he cometh
to judge the earth:
he shall judge
the world with righteousness,
and the people with his truth.

(PSALM 96, 9–13)

But our God
is in the heavens:
he hath done
whatsoever he hath pleased.
Their idols
are silver and gold,
the work of men's hands.
They have mouths,
but they speak not:
eyes have they,
but they see not:
they have ears,
but they hear not:
noses have they,
but they smell not:
they have hands,
but they handle not:
feet have they,
but they walk not:
neither speak they
through their throat.
They that make them
are like unto them;
so is everyone that trusteth
in them.

(PSALM 115, 3–8)

but immediately apprehensible to its recipient and which was to find its ultimate and unequivocal expression in the Ten Commandments of Sinai—delivered to a people upon whom they became binding. By recognizing one God only, from whom the moral law derived authority and sanctification, Israel created a superior synthesis of ethics and monotheism.

Israel's faith and history, through the covenant with God, were indissolubly conjoined in a union that the people's special form of life must essentially express.

In the early days of their settlement as a simple people of shepherds and peasants, it was a form of life that was virtually enforced by their existence as a confederation of independent tribes, united by their covenant with God and watched over by elders. But attacks upon them by the Philistines meant that a central military leadership was required and the need of the hour led to the installation of a king. Thus a conflict arose.

For by degrees monarchy led to the development of trade and a differentiated economy which destroyed the equality previously existing among the people and raised to power a rich upper caste which soon forgot the commandment of neighbourly love. Close contacts with adjacent peoples and interstate royal marriages inevitably led to the infiltration of alien cults. The tragic conflict between the need for survival in war and peace, which only a secular overlord could ensure, and a faith that demanded the sole authority of God, precipitated a series of religious crises from which the people emerged only by the grace of their prophets. Often enough it was against the monarch that these men, divinely inspired, raised their voices in warning and admonition.

In spite of a tradition going back for centuries, the monarchy was not restored when the people, determined to walk in godly ways, returned to their country from the Babylonian exile. Under tolerant Persian supremacy they were able to find a way of life suited to their particular character, and leadership was entrusted to their High Priest.

It was a way of life that isolated them from the rest of that world. Neighbouring peoples had the colourful myths of their pantheon, but Israel was already living in a real world governed by the strict law of her God. To other peoples, their gods were a source of inspiration in figurative art; Israel's God could not be represented. This was more than compensated for by the people's close I-Thou relationship with their God. It found artistic expression in music and poetry.

The difference between Israel and other peoples was a fateful one. She lost her country in saving her own culture from being engulfed by another, that of the Romans. But the vital strength of the people, under constant threat of convulsion, was rooted in the land promised to them by God, and the hope of return sustained them through all vicissitudes. Their faith, which was their heritage, went with them in the dispersion and saved monotheistic ethics both for them and for the world.

In his novel *Tancred,* Disraeli, the great protagonist of the British Empire in the Victorian era, says:

A race that persists
in celebrating their vintage,
although they have no
fruits to gather,
will regain their vineyards.

THE GARDEN OF EDEN

For centuries men have been preoccupied with the mystery of creation and with the place where the first human couple received the breath of life. The origin of existence is imaginatively expressed in myth, and every people has its own version. It is the more astonishing then to find how many elements are common to most legends: chaos is dispelled by a creative force; the first living being emerges from primeval waters; clay is the substance from which man is made.

There are two separate Biblical accounts belonging to different times, but which, in the minds of most people, tend to merge into a single story of creation. We remember Adam and Eve, the serpent, the tree of the knowledge of good and evil, the expulsion from the Garden of Eden; we also remember that God created the world in six days. But very few are aware that the story of Paradise was set down by a 'Jahvist' writer, probably as early as the ninth century B.C., while the account of the creation of the world in six days was recorded by a priest of the fifth century.

In the later account, which comes first in the Bible, God sets about his work carefully, with the deliberation of wisdom, divides heaven and earth, land and water, creates the stars of the night and day, makes plants and animals, and not until the earth is habitable and productive does he crown his achievement by creating a man and a woman who are to inherit the earth.

> And God blessed them, and God said unto them, be fruitful and
> multiply and replenish the earth, and subdue it.... (GENESIS I, 28)

The priestly document concludes with the consecration of the seventh day as a day of rest. There is no indication as to God's further intentions for his creatures. It is a grandiose cosmogony that is suggested here; creation takes place in the formlessness of the All, its product is the inhabited universe, its means a mere 'Let there be...', its object, Man.

The original Old Testament picture of creation is found to be interwoven with the naive ideas, the myth and folklore of the earlier account. How different is the picture painted by the Jahvist author from the priestly cosmogony! A vital, active God first forms man out of the dust of the ground, into which he breathes the breath of life, but only then does he create the conditions for him to live in. And we can almost see God as he plants trees—the Tree of Knowledge and the Tree of Life in the midst of Paradise, creates animals and arranges everything to ensure a sweet existence for the lonely man in the Garden of Eden. Finally, God produces a woman from Adam's rib, since there was no other suitable companion for the man. At last, man is commanded not to eat of the Tree of Knowledge:

> '...for in the day that thou eatest thereof, thou shalt surely die.'
> (GENESIS 2, 17)

What had to happen, did happen. Seduced by the serpent, the couple ate of the fruit

Nomads do not write their history, they tell it. Thus it came about that everything that happened to the People of Israel during their long years of wandering was for centuries handed down orally, and their history only began to be written when the people had become sedentary. But it was to be another few hundred years before the various parts of the inherited tradition were amalgamated to form the first part of the Old Testament comprized in the five Books of Moses, the Pentateuch. It is possible that the first versions were based on considerably earlier ones, for writing had been known in Mesopotamia in the fourth millennium B.C. But no such document has survived till later times, and the Bible remains the only source for Israel's early historical and religious development.

It is to Bible research in the literary-critical sense that we owe the discovery and identification of the various sources of the Pentateuch, the composition of which was ascribed by tradition to Moses alone. It was found that there were four distinct documentary sources, each based upon earlier, orally transmitted material and preceding sources, namely, the Jahvist (J), using the name 'Jahve' for God, whose authors belong to the ninth century B.C.; the Elohist (E), using the name 'Elohim' for God, and belonging to the eighth century; the Deuteronomist (D), of the seventh century, and the Priestly (P), whose authors compiled the 'Priestly Codes' in the fifth century, adding these to the Pentateuch to form a whole.

There were further refinements. But it was reserved for our time to contest the leading position of Biblical criticism in the field of research. This occurred as a result of progressive archaeological discoveries in the Near East from which it became increasingly evident that the Old Testament narrative can be related to the history and civilization of the ancient east. The stories of the Bible, formerly consigned to the realm of legend, have acquired unexpected weight as an historical source.

The story of the Tree of Knowledge is the myth of man's emulation of God. Loss of eternal life is the price paid by man for his thirst for the whole of knowledge, the possession of which is a divine prerogative.

Sumerian cylinder seal impression from the middle of the third millennium B.C. Even before writing was discovered there were seals (stamp seals), the first sign of possession, in southern Mesopotamia. In the glyptic (gem-cutting) art of cylinder seals, invented before 3,000, depth of engraving and skilled workmanship could produce images of enchanting loveliness and force of expression, vividly reflecting the early civilization of Mesopotamia.

Of the four 'Rivers of Paradise' only the Tigris (Hiddekel) and the Euphrates are known. Attempts have been made to identify the Gihon with the Nile and the Pison with the Persian Gulf. The concept probably originated in

Babylonian culture. In the Middle Ages, Christians liked to relate the Rivers of Paradise to the four gospels and the four cardinal virtues, Prudence, Courage, Temperance and Justice.

of the deadly tree; they passed heedlessly by the tree of life. For the serpent said to the woman:

> 'Ye shall not surely die: For God doth know that in the day ye eat thereof, then your eyes shall be opened, and ye shall be as gods, knowing good and evil.' (GENESIS 3, 5)

The account goes on to show how God, walking in the Garden of Eden in the cool of the evening, loses his temper in truly human fashion when he catches out the sinners: he curses the sinning trio, drives them out and sets angels to guard the closed gates of Paradise to prevent man eating of the tree of life and so obtaining eternal life as well as the knowledge of good and evil.

> And the Lord God said, Behold, the man is become as one of us....
> (GENESIS 3, 22)

That is, like one of the gods, whose multiplicity is recognized. Between the two accounts, then, lies the formation of the absolute concept of God which was to set its stamp upon, and determine the destiny of, the people of the Bible.

When God realizes that man prefers knowledge and independence to innocence and eternal happiness in Paradise, he feels pity for his creature now doomed to die. As a last loving act before their expulsion, God is shown providing our primeval ancestors with clothes:

> Unto Adam also and to his wife did the Lord God make coats of skins and clothed them. (GENESIS 3, 21)

He did no more. For very wisely he had made Adam and Eve out of the earth of Babylon, the land through which the Tigris and Euphrates flow, so that Paradise lay in a country fertile enough for man to find a living by the sweat of his brow.

And a river went out of Eden
to water the garden;
and from thence it was parted, and became into four heads.
The name of the first is Pison: that is it which compasseth
the whole land of Havilah,
where there is gold;
and the gold of that land is good:
there is bdellium and the onyx stone.
And the name of the second river is Gihon:
the same is it that compasseth the whole land of Ethiopia.
And the name of the third river is Hiddekel:
that is it which goeth toward the east of Assyria.
And the fourth river is Euphrates.

(GENESIS 2, 10–14)

And in fact traces of the earliest civilizations were found in Mesopotamia. For primitive cultures made their appearance there even before they did in Egypt—the other country to play a part in Israel's history.

THE HERITAGE OF PARADISE

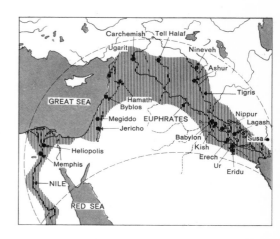

Early civilizations in the 'Fertile Crescent', a term designating the fertile regions of Egypt, Palestine, Syria and Mesopotamia. These lands were the seat of considerable civilizations at a time when Europe was still plunged·in darkness.

The fate of a country and of its people is determined by its rivers. Only where these exist can man slowly become independent of the hazards of hunting and food-gathering, domesticate animals, till the soil of the land, and become sedentary. But in order to create a new paradise on earth, he must learn to build dams and to dig canals, so that the horror of floods may be transformed into the blessing of irrigation.

The possession of great rivers, the Tigris and Euphrates, and the art of irrigation made of Mesopotamia a land of high civilization and culture long before the history of the people of the Bible began.

The difficult nature of irrigation and settlement in the southern region, Sumer, forced the people there to work together in an organized way and so determined the country's development. In the wide estuarine plain by the Persian Gulf the two rivers deposited large masses of silt which created large areas of swampland. Repeated deposits of silt in the same places led to the gradual development of islands. Ur was built on one of these islands, the 'Ur of the Chaldees', a city of wealth and importance long before Abraham's time. There were other towns built on islands, many of them known to us from the Bible and other sources, for instance Erech (Uruk), Babylon, Kish, Nippur and Eridu, the latter being regarded by the Sumerians, the inhabitants of the Biblical country of Shinar, as the oldest town in the world. As early as the beginning of the third millennium B.C. these towns became city-states ruled by priest-kings, 'delegates of heaven'. They had a chequered history, for Sumer was open on all sides and without protection either against invasion by land-hungry nomads or against military attack. Thus in 2350 B.C. the Semitic King Sargon I of Akkad was able to overthrow the early Sumerian dynasties and to found the Sumero-Akkadian empire—the first great empire in history. The city-states, however, attained their final synthesis only in the second Semitic empire of the Amorite king Hammurabi (1728–1686).

It was in south Mesopotamia that observation of heavenly bodies led to a knowledge of planetary orbits; that the earliest form of writing known to man, cuneiform, was evolved in its original hieroglyphic form in the fourth millennium B.C. in the service of the temple authorities, and the greatest epic poem to appear before Homer, the Gilgamesh Epic, was written down during the early Sumero-Akkadian era; that King Hammurabi collected the Sumerian and Semitic legal tradition into a system which is now regarded as the most important Mesopotamian legal code; that, in the third millennium, the art of gem-cutting (glyptic) was at its zenith.

Wherever Abraham and his kinsmen may have lived in Mesopotamia—the Bible mentions Ur as well as Haran as their habitat—and although as shepherds they only lived on the fringes of this high culture, it was inevitable that these semi-nomads should have felt the influence of urban civilization and culture. They had to go into the towns to obtain articles for everyday use, such as clay vessels, in exchange for their own products—animals, skins and wool. They certainly knew the local deities

The spade of the archaeologist has uncovered important village settlements in northern Mesopotamia, some dating back to the fifth millennium before Christ. It is not possible to say exactly which peoples lived there, but their artefacts, such as ceramics found at Tell Halaf, show technical and artistic skills not equalled until the Greeks, several millennia later.

Votive offering from early Sumerian times (beginning of the third millennium B.C.). Limestone figurine of a praying woman (from an excavation at Lagash).

How glorious is thy rising up
at heaven's rim
O living Aton,
source of life!
When thou risest
in the eastern firmament,
the whole land
is filled with thy beauty.
Beautiful art thou,
and great,
and shinest high
over all the land.
Thy rays embrace the lands
to the very ends
of thy creation.
Thou art Ra,
thou takest all men captive
with thy love
and compellest them
for thy beloved son.
Thou art far away
yet thy rays strike the earth
and the faces of men
reflect thine image.

From the *Sun Song* of Pharaoh Amenhotep IV (1378–1362 B.C.). In his religious reforms, he sought to eliminate all the other deities of Egypt and to set up Aton, the sun god, as the only god. This teaching found its purest expression in the hymn to the sun, presumably his community's cult song and very possibly composed by himself.

CAPTIONS TO COLOUR PLATES

Page 17: This fertility figure was made more than three millennia before Abraham's time (from an excavation near Beersheba).

Pages 18/19: The stony waste of the Negev desert, south of Beersheba.

Page 20: ... and flowers spring up in the desert after the rain ...

and would have worshipped them. There were hundreds, both high gods—the seven gods who determine fate—and lesser deities. The high gods (such as the mighty Enlil, the moon god Nannar, the vegetation god Tammuz, the goddess of love, Ishtar) were provided with magnificent temples on raised terraces in the middle of a sacred precinct with walls to exclude the ordinary mortal. For this reason, in the second millennium, townsmen began to build small sanctuaries among the maze of streets in their cities, where lesser deities might be worshipped without hindrance and their intercession with the high gods prayed for. Nothing was visible of the temple precincts but the huge stepped tower (the ziggurat), unmistakably pointing heavenward. For young Abraham, in his search for God, this may have been one of his earliest impressions.

Egypt, too, owes her historical development and early appearance in the history of culture to her river. But the land in which this people and culture evolved was unlike Mesopotamia. The flooding of the Tigris and Euphrates was irregular, depending upon the thaw in the mountains of Armenia, but the flooding of the Nile was a regular and even calculable phenomenon, which led to the observation of the stars and to the reckoning of the first calendar. Again, Mesopotamia had no defined frontiers and was therefore defenceless against invasion, while Egypt was cut off to both east and west by huge desert tracts and to the south by the rapids of the First Cataract, which only permitted the infiltration of outside elements in numbers small enough to be easily absorbed. To this naturally isolated position Egypt owed an historical continuity impossible to Mesopotamia. And while in Mesopotamia dynasties and city-states were still struggling for supremacy, Egypt already had a single ruler by the beginning of the third millennium. This was the Pharaoh Menes who, by unifying Upper and Lower Egypt, gave the country political stability.

In Mesopotamia it was the moon that was accorded special adoration, but in Egypt it was the sun. The Pharaoh was not, as in Mesopotamia, the delegate of god, but himself a sun deity, the visible embodiment of Horus, the falcon and sun god. Costly burial places, which reached the height of their magnificence in the pharaonic pyramids, were symbols of an unqualified faith in survival after death.

The annual flooding of the Nile brought fertility and plenty to Egypt; she produced five times more than her own needs, and in ancient times she was the world's granary.

This was why Abraham, as we learn from the Bible, looked to Egypt for help during a time of famine in Canaan. But his descendants, the children of Israel, were later to experience in Egypt the never-to-be-forgotten bitterness of slavery. God's dialogues with Moses reflect their sufferings. To us the people are but a faceless, inarticulate multitude. The time during which the children of Israel grew in strength in spite of oppression is a time of uncanny silence, with but one reverberation: 'For we were bondsmen in the land of Egypt....'

The children of Israel were little influenced in other respects by the culture of Egypt. The very fact that they were shepherds, and as such held in utter contempt by the Egyptians, would have precluded them from participating in it even before their bondage. And the deification of a man, Pharaoh, must have been an abomination to people who had abjured the world of polytheism. It must be assumed that the two peoples regarded each other as barbarians, but for different reasons.

THE FIRST EXODUS

And Terah took Abram his son, and Lot
the son of Haran his son's son, and Sarai
his daughter in law, his son Abram's wife;
and they went forth with them from Ur of the Chaldees,
to go into the land of Canaan;
and they came unto Haran and dwelt there.

(GENESIS 11, 31)

This piece of information, terse and quite unexpected, is the first mention in the Bible of the land of Canaan as the goal of the migration and Haran in northern Mesopotamia as a stopping place on the way there. The region between these two areas was to be the stage for the first act of a long drama, but Ur is scarcely mentioned again.

Nothing has so deeply influenced the course of history as the wanderings of nomads driven by the desire to settle. Towards the end of the third millenium B.C. the Semitic 'Amurru' (Amorites) began to stream from the west into the cultivated land of the Near East where they formed the basis of the later Mesopotamian Amorite kingdoms of Mari and Babylon. At about the same time they overran the land of Canaan which was named *Amurru* after them. In 1950 B.C. the third dynasty of Ur collapsed under the pressure of the Elamite invasion from the east. It may have been the destruction of the towns of Ur and the upheavals resulting from it that drove the small pastoral kinship of Terah to emigrate. That the early history of the patriarchs is rooted in that of the Near East becomes evident if, following the Bible, we consider Terah's and Abraham's departure from Chaldea. Progressive archaeological discoveries in Canaan which enable us to place the first conquests of the land by the children of Israel in the second half of the thirteenth century B.C. would seem to put the Patriarchate at about the sixteenth or fifteenth century B.C. There are no documents other than the Bible concerning this time.

But did this kinship in fact ever live in the region of Ur? There is no evidence for this. Only the mythological tale of the flood which has a parallel in the Sumerian Gilgamesh Epic point to their having lived in Sumeria, Shinar in the Bible. A comparison of the two stories is of some interest. Utnapishtim, the Sumerian Noah, is the only survivor of a disastrous flood caused by the caprice of the gods; but the flood of the Bible is God's punishment for the wickedness of men which became almost immediately manifest in the early days of creation in Cain's murder of his brother.

But yesterday's myth is the truth of today. During excavations at Ur and other Sumerian towns a level layer of sediment about ten feet thick was uncovered which contained no ceramic remains, while beneath it there was another layer containing potsherds. Modern methods of archaeological research led to the conclusion that the population had in fact fallen victim to a local flood disaster in the fourth millennium B.C., and it could well be that stories of floods retain a memory of the tremendous inundations after the last Ice Age.

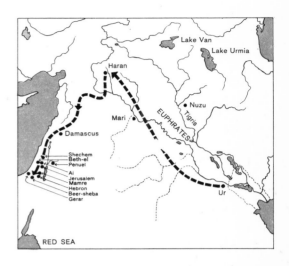

The Book of Genesis tells how the small pastoral family of Terah migrated from Ur of the Chaldees to settle in Haran, and how the patriarch Abraham was commanded by God to leave his tribe, taking his close family with him, and go to Canaan, the land that God had promised him.

And it came to pass
after these things,
that it was told Abraham,
saying,
Behold, Milcah, she hath
also born children
unto thy brother Nahor.

(GENESIS 22, 20)

There is no clear indication in the Bible as to the original habitat of Terah's family. Thus Nahor, one of his sons, lived in the region of Haran, the Biblical Aram-naharaim, although he is not mentioned amongst those who left Ur for Haran. One of Nahor's sons is Bethuel, the father of Rebekah who is fetched from Haran to become Isaac's wife; but Genesis 11, 28 states that: 'Haran died before his father Terah in the land of his nativity, in Ur of the Chaldees'! We can do no more than consider Mesopotamia to be the home of the family in the widest sense and Aram-Naharaim (Haran) as the centre where they settled down.

Ruins of the Biblical Haran. This town is of crucial significance in the history of the People of Israel, for it provides archaeological confirmation of the Biblical account. Excavations in the small Assyrian town of Nuzu—near what is today Kirkuk in Iraq and to the south-east of what is now Haran—have brought to light a temple and a palace from the time of the Mitannian kingdom (fifteenth century B.C.), as well as many cuneiform clay tablets of which the text describes customs in the east in the second millennium B.C. that are already familiar to us

There are, however, conclusive proofs that the tribe settled in Haran. The names Terah, Serug and Nahor given in the family tree (GENESIS 11, 10ff.) have survived up till the present in place-names such as Tell Nachuri (Nahor's Hill) and Tell Turachi (Terah's Hill). Documents found at Nuzu in northern Mesopotamia show remarkable agreement between the laws of inheritance, concubinage and adoption and the usage of the patriarchs. The clay tablets from Mari on the middle Euphrates contain so large a number of west Semitic words that it would seem that their language was identical with that of the ancient Hebrew of the patriarchs.

from Biblical stories. The deathbed blessing (GENESIS 27), the custom of ensuring an heir by means of concubines (GENESIS 16; 30), relationships such as those between Jacob and Laban (GENESIS 29; 31), the role of 'teraphim' (household gods) in inheritance (GENESIS 31, 19–34) are found in the light of archaeological discoveries to be authentic features of life at the time of the patriarchs.

... and all the first-born of man among thy children shalt thou redeem (buy off).
(EXODUS 13, 13).

Statuette of shepherd with sacrificial lamb (Sumerian, end of third millennium B.C., excavated at Mari).

At that time, Haran was a flourishing trading city on the caravan route between Mesopotamia and Egypt. It was also the centre of moon worship, to which Terah adhered. It cannot be supposed that the guardians of the temple precincts, who forbade entry to the Sumerian citizen, should react more kindly to the pious wishes of nomadic shepherds. It is all the more comprehensible that Abraham should seek a personal and approachable God.

According to the legend, Terah made small idols which one day were broken by Abraham. This was a revolution. Abraham spoke of God. And God spoke to him.

Now the Lord had said unto Abram, Get thee out of thy country, and from thy kindred, and from thy father's house, unto a land that I will show thee. And I will make of thee a great nation.... And I will bless them that bless thee, and curse him that curseth thee: and in thee shall all families of the earth be blessed. So Abram departed, as the Lord had spoken unto him; and Lot went with him: And Abram took Sarai his wife, and Lot his brother's son, and all their substance they had gathered, and the souls that they had gotten in Haran; and they went forth, to go into the land of Canaan. (GENESIS 12, 1–3, 5)

This Biblical account interrupts the catalogue of genealogies; up to that point all the tribes—later the peoples—arise out of the story of the creation. Beyond it, attention is concentrated exclusively on the fate of this one group of shepherds from whose anonymity Abraham emerges as a clearly defined personality.

The kinship of Abraham was semi-nomadic, and like many other tribes of that time, they were seeking lands in which to settle. Terah and all the others who stayed behind became sedentary at Haran, but Abraham followed his star.

Semi-nomadic life was very different from the later unlimited freedom of the Bedouin who, with their fast camels, could make a sudden surprise attack on another tribe and seize their cattle. The camel is tough, able to exist for days on end in the desert without water, and serves the Bedouin as a beast of burden, a mount and also as food. But before the camel was domesticated, in about 1100 B.C., the pastoral nomad relied on the donkey as a mount and load-carrier. Riding from pasturage to pasturage, camping in the south during the winter and spring and in the north during the summer, he would come to an agreement with a peasant whose fields had been harvested and where his herds could graze. He could never move far from cultivated land, and certainly would not have been able to cross large tracts of desert since donkeys cannot go without water for very long.

After their departure from Haran, life became very much more difficult for Abraham's little band. They travelled southwards. It was unknown territory, not so fertile or so well watered as northern Mesopotamia; painfully they made their way from oasis to oasis until they came to the land that God would show them.

THE LAND OF CANAAN

Finding water was the problem that confronted the small group of people who went with Abraham to Canaan, and the digging of wells was their first act of civilization. A very long time afterwards, when Abraham's descendants, the children of Israel, came to take possession of the land God had promised them, the knowledge of cistern building, acquired and developed during an unusually prolonged existence as nomads, stood them in good stead. Archaeology ascribes to them a highly evolved technique in this field which, indeed, enabled

Canaan, the Biblical name for the Syrian and Palestinian region along the eastern Mediterranean, was a long, narrow belt of country rugged with mountain ranges between which the Orontes in the north and the Jordan in the south had carved deep valleys. Beyond the eastern border was the Syrian Desert, and in the south the Negev (Southland), the country's desert, merged imperceptibly into the vast desert areas of Arabia and the Sinai peninsula.

Most of nature's gifts had fallen to the northern part of the land. It derived importance from its position as a link between the great political and economic powers of Mesopotamia and Egypt. Both those countries lacked timber, which made the cedars of Lebanon in north Canaan a coveted possession. Both countries were short of seaports, but north Canaan had deep bays, allowing the development of busy ports—Ugarit, Byblos and Sidon—so that the inhabitants of the coast, the Phoenicians, became one of the most important trading and colonizing peoples of the ancient world.

The principal caravan routes linking the three continents, Europe, Asia and Africa, met in Canaan, which became the cockpit where the rival powers struggled for influence. Ever since the time of her Old Kingdom (c. 2700–2220 B.C.) Egypt had enjoyed supremacy over the country, a supremacy that at first had been economic rather than political. And when in the sixteenth century B.C. the Hittite kingdom, and in the fifteenth the Hurrian kingdom of Mitanni, and later still Assyria, entered the lists of power politics, the peoples of Canaan were seldom masters in their own country, which was constantly being overrun by the armies of the great powers. In addition, the cultivated land exercised a strong attraction on the nomads of Arabia and the Sinai peninsula.

The flat, sandy coast of the south had only two ports of any significance: Joppa (Jaffa) and Accho (Acre). The broad plain of Jezreel that stretched right across the country along the foothills of the Mountains of Galilee to the Mediterranean, the coastal plains, part of the Jordan valley and the oases to the north of the Dead Sea, were all fertile. South Canaan was a land of great contrasts, both in appearance and in climate, a land with too much and too little, cold enough for snow in the high, windy mountains walling in the valleys, oppressively hot in the Jordan depression, like a furnace round about the Dead Sea, the deepest natural depression in the world descending to some thirteen hundred feet below sea level. The *wadis* (river valleys) between the mountains, which in summer were dry, became swollen in winter by sudden rainstorms and turned into raging torrents. Even in late spring hot sandstorms from the desert shrivelled every living plant.

It was precisely this geographical situation, with so varied and changeable a character and climate, that largely determined the destiny of the Canaanite peoples.

> And into the land of Canaan they came. And Abram passed through
> the land unto the place of Sichem, unto the plain of Morah. And the
> Canaanite was then in the land. (GENESIS 12, 5–6)

them to settle in the hitherto almost unoccupied uplands of Canaan, where they found sufficient grazing for their beasts.

These early settlers found new tasks confronting them when it became necessary to defend their territory against hostile immigration, and to conquer new lands for their growing population, Israel being a healthy pastoral race, in the plains occupied by the Canaanites. The irregularity and wildness peculiar to this country, by separating one tribe from another, made it difficult to assemble men for war; lack of weapons reduced them to guerilla warfare which was only effective in close country fighting and safe under cover of darkness.

Canaan was peculiarly difficult to conquer and to hold because the varied nature of its landscape demanded both close combat and open warfare in the plains, the latter requiring not so much skill as up-to-date equipment for a successful outcome. An intimate knowledge of the terrain in the mountains permitting the full use of available cover brought Israel repeated successes against enemies greatly superior both in arms and in numbers whose cumbersome war chariots were useless there. But as a tactical device the chariots made the Canaanites invincible in the plain, in open battle. It was not until Israel had equality of armament to add to her experience of guerilla warfare that she was gradually able to invade the fertile lowlands and take possession of the whole country. Plate: The Jordan.

THE PEOPLES BY THE WAY

Canaanite woman of Megiddo (c. 1200 B.C.). The Canaanites were superior to the children of Israel in all the civilized attainments, as objets d'art of ivory (see above), alabaster and gold from Canaanite excavations testify.

And Canaan begat Sidon
his first-born,
and Heth, and the Jebusite,
and the Amorite, and the Girgasite,
and the Hivite, and the Arkite,
and the Sinite, and the Arvadite,
and the Zemarite, and the Hamathite;
and afterward were the families
of the Canaanites spread abroad.

(GENESIS 10, 15–18)

Of all the peoples mentioned—Sidon, Canaan and Heth just as though they were personal names—only those who founded kingdoms of some size left behind monuments and written texts: the Hittites in Asia Minor, the Hurrites (the Biblical Horites), in their kingdom of Mitanni, the Amorites in Mari and Babylon on the central and lower Euphrates and also in Amurru (Canaan). All the rest disappeared without trace in the process of ethnic assimilation. Of the Jebusites, we only know that they lived in Jebus (Jerusalem) and the Hivites are believed to have lived in the town of Gibeon. In Canaan, the Amorites (Amurru) became entirely assimilated with the local population, the Canaanites. The country derived its name from Canaanite, or 'dealer in purple dyes'.

The names Canaan and Phoenicia mean approximately *Land of Purple*; the coast was the habitat of the murex from which the dye came. Phoenicians and Canaanites were, as we have already seen, one and the same people—they not only lived in the same geographical area, but they had the same cultural and linguistic tradition; and up till the fifth century A.D. in Punic Carthage, which had been founded by the Phoenicians, the Canaanite origins of the people were still a matter of pride. The Canaanite-Phoenician dialect belongs to the north-west Semitic group of languages.

It is certain that the land was settled by Canaanites as far back as the second millennium B.C., but it seems probable that settlement had already taken place in the third millennium.

Our first knowledge of the religion and customs of the Canaanites derives from the work of a Greek, Philo of Byblos, who wrote a history of Phoenicia in the first century A.D. But the excavation in this century of Ugarit, the Canaanite port, cast an entirely new light on what was known of the country's culture. The discovery and deciphering of the Ugarit cuneiform texts to a large extent confirmed Philo's account.

As everywhere throughout the ancient world, religion dominated the life and thoughts of these peoples, and the Canaanite deities who represented the forces of nature were nature gods expressed in human terms. They already showed characteristics of the later Greek pantheon. For while the gods of the Mesopotamian heaven—apart from the inevitable struggle between Marduk, the supreme god and creator of the universe, and Tiamat, the goddess of chaos—had a certain dignity and glamour, the Canaanite deities were barbaric, bloodthirsty and lascivious; in other words, their nature was distinctly sensual. The Canaanite religion, then, was palpably closer to the primordial idea of deities than that of their far more civilized Mesopotamian contemporaries.

The composition of the heavenly hierarchy varied with each individual town. But as the particular nature of their deities and the relationships between them did not generally lend themselves to hard and fast definition they were usually able to fit in to the overall Canaanite pantheon. The hierarchy about which we know most is that of Ugarit. El, father of gods and men, lived 'a thousand valleys and a thousand fields' away from Canaan, 'at the source of the two rivers, among the springs of the two deeps', in a cosmic paradise, that is, where the gods must seek him out to hear his advice. He was a bloodthirsty tyrant who dethroned his father and castrated him, sliced off his daughter's head and offered up 'his one and only son' as a sacrifice to his father. According to Philo, one of El's daughters was the virgin Anath, sister and wife of Baal. Baal seized El's throne, as Zeus seized that of Chronos, and became the principal god in the Canaanite pantheon.

It is not always easy to follow the changing relationships of the goddesses to the gods El and Baal or to determine their ambiguous character. They were all mother goddesses and also heavenly courtesans. Anath and Astarte were the goddesses who 'receive but do not bear'. It is precisely in the role of courtesan that they are called sacred—*kudshu*. The fertility goddess Astarte, like Anath, was also goddess of war and often bloodthirsty and savage. We are told of an appalling massacre of young men wrought by Anath who 'waded up to the neck in blood'.

The centre of the Canaanite mythological stage is held by the figures of Baal and Anath, deities of a totally unrestrained fertility cult. Another central theme is the bloody strife between the god of death Mot, Baal's enemy, and Anath who snatches his victims from him. In the Canaanite cult 'sacral union' played an important role in the rite of temple prostitution. It was magic, practised to ensure the reawakening of nature, and to render productive all human activity.

The gods were offered sacrifices in magnificent shrines beside sacred springs, but especially in high places, in order to entreat their favour, to thank them, to reconcile them or to avert imminent disaster. Archaeological finds thereabouts have shown that not only animals were sacrificed but also humans. The Bible even tells of child sacrifice to Moloch in the Hinnom Valley near Jerusalem. Underneath houses of the Canaanite era clay vessels containing skeletons of children have been discovered. The same kind of gruesome objects have been found in the sanctuary of Tanit near Carthage, suggesting that this cruel cult was practised until late antiquity.

The usual process accompanying invasion by nomads was their adoption of the higher culture of the new country and the amalgamation of their pantheon with that of the indigenous people. This was made easier by the fact that the gods of antiquity generally represented the forces of nature and in the eyes of nomads the deities of a fertile, settled country would seem more open-handed than their own.

And Abraham said
unto his eldest servant
of his house,
that ruled over all that he had,
Put, I pray thee,
thy hand under my thigh:
And I will make thee swear
by the Lord,
the God of heaven,
and the God of the earth,
that thou shalt not take a wife
unto my son
of the daughters
of the Canaanites,
among whom I dwell:
But thou shalt go
unto my country,
and to my kindred,
and take a wife
unto my son Isaac.

(GENESIS 24, 2–4)

DEITIES AND GOD

The idea of gods and demons, both of which stem from one source, goes back to the earliest history of man when he was still leading an unstable, wandering life surrounded by countless dangers. Every object was to him a being, his world was peopled with spirits whose malevolence he sought to allay by incantations and whose favour he courted, for instance, by shooting arrows at the picture of a quarry which he thus magically killed. The belief that influence could be thus transferred persisted into a late stage of religious development, but with increasing insight and experience, man's concept of God changed; he saw the world of the gods in the light of what he knew about his own.

He also ascribed to the gods the same difference of rank as existed in human society. From this mass of supernatural beings he elected some to be high gods representing the forces of nature to whose power he was subject. Like humans, the gods also had family ties and generated life, and in the same way that the father is the head of the human family, the head of the heavenly hierarchy was a father-figure. But the father-figure did not occupy the central position in the world of mythology; this was taken by a young, vital god, the god of vegetation. When the countryside withered, this

This Biblical passage shows the special place held by the 'eldest servant' (perhaps Eliezer) in Abraham's household. Abraham and Sarah had probably followed a custom of the time in taking him in place of a child, for Abraham expresses the fear (GENESIS 15, 2) that 'this Eliezer of Damascus' will possess his house should God fail to give him an heir of his own.

The passage proves how scrupulously God's command not to intermarry with Canaanites was obeyed. But only a generation later there was a different attitude, and we are told:

And Esau (one of the two sons of Isaac) was forty years old when he took to wife Judith the daughter of Beeri the Hittite, and Bashemath, the daughter of Elon the Hittite. 'Which were a grief of mind unto Isaac and to Rebekah'. (GENESIS 26, 34–35)

It is true that to please his parents Esau also married Mahalath, the daughter of Ishmael (son of Abraham and Hagar); but subsequently the descendants of the patriarchs gradually and inevitably mixed with the peoples of Canaan.

signified his death; when nature bloomed again, it signified the resurrection of the young god, whom the goddess of love had snatched away from the god of death. Man mourned the death of the young god and celebrated his resurrection in an orgiastic ritual. In the union of god and goddess he saw the necessary preliminary for the renewal of nature, and being convinced from primeval times that the course of events can be influenced by imitative magic, he believed that the 'sacral union' between king and priestess could bring about the same result. This was how man understood the yearly cycle, feeling himself part of a harmonious world whose course was determined by his nature gods.

The God of Israel was different, a new kind of god altogether. He was not the supreme head of any family, nor was he a part of the nature he had created. He stood transcendent, above nature and her laws, and outside her power. He was not bound up with the growth and dying away of vegetation, but while abolishing the fevered joys of the rites connected with the mythical pantheon's annual festival, he gave man the moral law which, if obeyed, entailed his blessing. A stern, demanding God, exacting renunciation, had come into men's lives, directing them towards a final condition in which life would be purified and hallowed.

THE PATRIARCHS AND THEIR WANDERING

Abraham believed in the omnipotence of his God. And God made a covenant with him.

And it came to pass, that,
when the sun went down and it was dark,
behold a smoking furnace, and a burning lamp
that passed between those pieces (sacrificial animals).
In the same day the Lord made a covenant
with Abram, saying,
Unto thy seed have I given this land,
from the river of Egypt unto the great river,
the river Euphrates....

(GENESIS 15, 17–18)

ABRAHAM COUNTS THE STARS

And he (the Lord) brought him forth abroad, and said, Look now toward heaven, and tell the stars, if thou be able to number them: and he said unto him, So shall thy seed be. And he believed in the Lord; and he counted it to him for righteousness.
(GENESIS 15, 5–6)

Relief on the bronze door in the west porch of the Basilica San Zeno in Verona (end of the eleventh century).

In the ancient east, this was the common form of contract between partners who had no knowledge of writing; it demanded that they pass between dismembered sacrificial animals as they were burning. The flames of the fire represented the covenant-making god. The cutting up of sacrificial animals is still reflected in present Hebrew usage with the expression *lachrot brith*—to 'cut' a contract. As a sign of the covenant, God demands circumcision—a custom widely practised in the ancient east—and this extends even to servants, whether 'born in thy house, or bought with money of any stranger, which is not of thy seed' as the Bible has it.

From Sichem, Abraham went still further south, probably in search of unoccupied land.

> And he removed from thence unto a mountain on the east of Beth-el, and pitched his tent, having Beth-el on the west, and Hai on the east: and there he builded an altar unto the Lord, and called upon the name of the Lord. And Abram journeyed, going on still toward the south. (GENESIS 12, 8–9)

Excavations have been made at Hai as well as at Beth-el, but it is probable that the 'altar' was only a stone raised in a place that inspired particular awe by a nomad in pious remembrance of his God—as was done also by Abraham's grandson Jacob who, after his dream of the ladder to heaven, dedicated the stone on which he had been resting and called the place Beth-el (House of God). The cult of the sacred stone was practised throughout Canaan, a significant proof of the close relationship between the religious customs of the patriarchs and those of the new country.

> And there was a famine in the land: and Abram went down into Egypt to sojourn there; for the famine was grievous in the land. (GENESIS 12, 10)

All the sacred places of the patriarchs—Sichem, Beth-el, Mamre, Beer-sheba—lay on the border between desert and cultivated land, an area in which there were sufficient watering-places for small livestock. But if the winter rains failed or came late, the land often suffered from famine. The nomads migrated to Egypt, a land they believed to be always fertile. Abraham, too, was drawn by the land of grain.

In Egypt he made out that Sarah was his sister. The theme of the wife-sister is found in the laws of the ancient world, those of the Hurrians, for instance, which give better protection to a woman who adds the status of sister—even without blood ties—to that of wife. In view of such genuine historical features in the Biblical tradition, the extremely lifelike and vivid descriptions of a pastoral existence or the candid delineation of the protagonists, the suggestion that the patriarchs are idolized ancestors or mythological figures would seem to be unfounded. These are human beings who are portrayed, driven by love and hate, by hunger, desire and the thirst for revenge, human beings who fail or else prove themselves when faced with decisions presented to them by God between good and evil, obedience and disobedience.

Abraham withstands the test when he leads his only, and so long and ardently desired, son Isaac to the place of sacrifice. But the voice of God—which today would be called an inner voice—prevents him from carrying out the ritual of a barbaric cult. This unique story of the sacrifice of Isaac symbolizes the departure from the sacrifice of the first-born, in whose place an animal is offered up.

Abraham was a respected tribal prince, and the blessing of his God showed itself in the increase of his property and of his power. Abraham was thus able to hasten to the assistance of the kings of the Dead Sea cities—Sodom, Gomorrah, Adama, Zeboim and Bela—with three hundred and eighteen men-at-arms. After a victorious retributive battle against Chedorlaomer and his Mesopotamian allies, Abraham released his nephew, Lot, from their imprisonment.

The story of the 'War of the Kings' certainly has an historical nucleus of truth, although neither the names of the kings nor the time of the war can be identified. Archaeological research has shown that the southern end of the Dead Sea covers what

And he (the angel) said, Lay not thine hand upon the lad... for now I know that thou fearest God.... (GENESIS 22, 12)

Abraham and Isaac. The story of these two patriarchs shows Abraham in his part of protector, which he exercises until well into Isaac's maturity. Isaac, the son of his old age, had as a child very nearly been offered up in sacrifice. To secure the whole inheritance for his son, Abraham sent away his seven other sons out of the land; Isaac was not even allowed to sue for his own bride, a task entrusted to Eliezer (GENESIS 24); he brings Isaac Bethuel's daughter, Rebekah.

Sculpture at the north entrance to Chartres Cathedral (early thirteenth century).

used to be the Valley of Siddim, the site of the cities Sodom and Gomorrah. These and the other three towns were destroyed in an earthquake about 1900 B.C. and were then covered by the waters of the Dead Sea.

> And the King of Sodom went out to meet him after his return from the slaughter of Chedorlaomer, and of the kings that were with him at the valley of Shaveh which is the king's dale. And Melchizedek king of Salem (Jerusalem) brought forth bread and wine: and he was the priest of the most high God. And he blessed him, and said, Blessed be Abram of the most high God, possessor of heaven and earth: And blessed be the most high God, which hath delivered thine enemies into thy hand. And he gave him tithes of all. (GENESIS 14, 17–22)

What did Melchizedek mean when he spoke of 'the most high God'?

The patriarchs retained possession of the field near Mamre—in the neighbourhood of Hebron—together with the cave of Machpelah which Abraham bought of the Hittite Ephron as a burial place. But there was no definite or final settlement. The patriarchs remained strangers among the peoples of Canaan.

Among the patriarchs fidelity to the tribe meant that their sons must seek wives in the former settlements of their family.

> And Isaac called Jacob, and blessed him, and charged him, and said unto him, Thou shalt not take a wife of the daughters of Canaan. Arise, go to Padan-aram, to the house of Bethuel thy mother's father; and take thee a wife from thence of the daughters of Laban thy mother's brother. (GENESIS 28, 1–2)

As Isaac had wooed Laban's sister Rebekah, of Haran, so his son, Jacob wed Laban's daughters, Leah and Rachel. But Isaac's son Esau took Hittite wives.

The Old Testament does not disguise the fact that Sarah induced her husband to drive out his Egyptian maid Hagar and her son Ishmael into the desert, so that the latter should not share Isaac's inheritance. When Jacob bought the birthright of his brother Esau it was probably a case of 'ultimogeniture', whereby the youngest, not the eldest, son is regarded as heir. Yet in the story of Isaac's blessing, the behaviour of Jacob and his mother is not condoned. The Bible repeatedly relates events which recur from generation to generation. Like Lot, Isaac too went to fresh pastures. As hunger had driven Abraham to Egypt, so Isaac also set forth to go there but, warned by God, remained in Gerar, the land of the Philistine king Abimelech. And like his father Abraham, who set up his tents there and dug wells, so too Isaac, driven out by Abimelech, dug wells at his new dwelling-place Beer-sheba, 'well of the oath'.

Israel came into existence as a people with Jacob, son of Isaac. After wrestling all night with the messenger of God—'I will not let thee go, except thou bless me'—he won the name of *Israel*, 'soldier of God'. 'And Jacob called the name of the place Peniel'—'God's face'.

It is remarkable how protracted and gradual was the development of the kinship. Of Abraham's sons, only Isaac remained in Canaan. Isaac's son Esau also had to seek his fortune outside the country. Only the twelve sons of Jacob, the third and last of the patriarchs, became the tribal ancestors of the later People of Israel. At this point the Bible narrative takes a leap forward, attributing to Jacob words of blessing reminiscent of a much later time, that of the Judges, which here give the impression of being a prophetic vision of his sons' destiny.

And Sarah was an hundred and seven and twenty years old:
these were the years of the life of Sarah.
And Sarah died in Kirjath-arba;
the same is in Hebron in the land of Canaan;
and Abraham came to mourn for Sarah,
and to weep for her.
And Abraham stood up from before his dead,
and spake unto the sons of Heth, saying:
I am a stranger and a sojourner with you;
give me a possession
of a buryingplace with you,
that I may bury my dead out of my sight...
hear me, and intreat for me
to Ephron the son of Zohar,
that he may give me the cave of Machpelah,
which he hath,
which is in the end of his field;
for as much money as it is worth...
and Ephron the Hittite answered...
Nay, my lord, hear me:
the field give I thee,
and the cave that is therein,
I give it thee....
(GENESIS 23, 1–4, 8–11)

This kind of transaction, typical of the oriental, gives the deal the pleasing aspect of an exchange of presents, the return gift being the price that is paid.

The tombs of Abraham and Sarah, of Isaac and Rebekah and also of Jacob and Leah, built above the cave of Machpelah, are still shown to visitors in a mosque at Ramat el-Khalil (ancient Hebron). The cave itself, in which their remains are supposed to lie, has not been entered for hundreds of years, but was opened to visitors just recently.

IN THE LAND OF GOSHEN

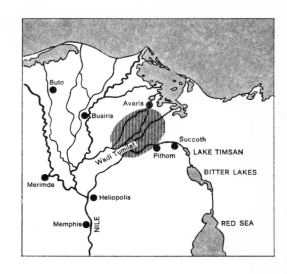

The fertile region of Wadi Tumilat was the Biblical Goshen, where Jacob and his sons settled.

The story of Joseph and his brethren introduces the history of the children of Israel's settlement in the eastern Nile delta—in Goshen. Joseph was Jacob's (Israel's) eleventh son and Rachel's first. 'Now Israel loved Joseph more than all his children....' (GENESIS 37, 3). His father's favourite, and dreamer of ambitious dreams, he aroused the hatred of his brothers. They humiliated him and sold their brother as a slave. And Joseph was carried off to Egypt. 'But the Lord was with Joseph, and showed him mercy....' Joseph withstood the blandishments of his mistress, who wished to seduce him. Slandered by her, he was thrown into prison. But his gift of interpreting dreams procured his freedom. Pharaoh, impressed by Joseph's interpretation of his dreams and by his intelligence, 'set him over all the land of Egypt'. As governor, Joseph laid in stores of food during the seven plenteous years—his interpretation of Pharaoh's dream of the seven well-fleshed kine and full ears—for the seven lean years, which had appeared to Pharao in the form of lean kine and empty ears. Joseph thus preserved Egypt from famine which threatened even the 'world's granary' if the Nile failed to rise high enough for several years in succession.

'And all countries came into Egypt to Joseph to buy corn, because that the famine was so sore in all lands.' Joseph's brothers, too, came from Canaan. One of the most moving passages to be found in the Bible is that in which Joseph, the man of power, makes himself known to his brothers. And in the words spoken by Joseph to his brothers we learn the theme of the last story of the patriarchs.

> But as for you, ye thought evil against me; but God meant it unto good, to bring to pass as it is this day, to save much people alive. (GENESIS 50, 20)

The story of Joseph—although the figure remains historically obscure—is true in many respects of life in Egypt at that time. The Amarna tablets of the fourteenth century B.C. inform us that during that period Semites held high offices of state. In Genesis 47, 13–23, there is a realistic account of how, in times of drought, small-holdings fall to the crown and finally the impoverished freeman loses his freedom to the Pharaoh. From a later Egyptian text (the Anastasi VI papyrus), we also hear of shepherds seeking entry into the eastern Nile delta 'so as to preserve themselves and their herds in the king's domain'. This region, the fertile 'Wadi Tumilat', is the Biblical Goshen where Jacob and his sons settled.

> And Joseph died, and all his brethren, and all that generation. And the children of Israel were fruitful, and increased abundantly, and multiplied, and waxed exceeding mighty; and the land was filled with them. Now there arose up a new king over Egypt, which knew not Joseph. And he said unto his people, Behold, the people of the

In 1887 a peasant woman happened to find a number of clay tablets in Tell el-Amarna, the central Egyptian town of residence of Amenhotep IV (Akhenaten). Her find led to the discovery of a voluminous correspondence, mostly between the Pharaohs Amenhotep III and IV and their governors and the more or less independent city princes in Canaan. These letters

of the fourteenth century B.C. are in Akkadian, the diplomatic language of the time in the Near East, and throw light on the historical background of the land of Canaan before it was taken by the Israelite tribes. Most of the small but strongly fortified towns were ruled by their own native prince and generally had besides an Egyptian overseer who was responsible for the collection of tribute, the security of trade routes and in some cases probably for the maintenance of a small garrison. Some of the writings have traces of Canaanite speech current at the time and are the earliest examples we have of that country's language.

Granite statue of Ramses II (1290–1224 B.C.). It was probably during his reign that the exodus of the children of Israel from Egypt took place.

Miraculous escapes by children destined for greatness are the subject of legends throughout the world. Sargon I of Akkad, founder of the Sumero-Akkadian kingdom, and Gilgamesh, the king of Erech in Sumer, had both suffered the same fate as Moses when they were small.

The derivation of the name Moses is not certain. In Egyptian it would mean 'child, son' (as in Tuthmosis, Kamosis, Ramses), but in Hebrew 'he who draws something out'.

children of Israel are more and mightier than we.... Therefore they did set over them taskmasters to afflict them with their burdens. And they built for Pharaoh treasure cities, Pithom and Raamses. (EXODUS I, 6–9, 11)

What had happened? The children of Israel were felt to be a threat to Egypt and as slaves were made to do forced labour. We know little more than these basic facts. As we have already said, the time during which the children of Israel were gathering strength in spite of their oppression was a time of uncanny silence....

Today there is a tendency to regard Ramses II (1290–1224 B.C.), one of the greatest builders of all time, as the Pharaoh of the oppression, the one who 'knew not Joseph', and to see Joseph himself as governor under Seti I (1308–1290 B.C.), Ramses II's father and predecessor. Excavations of the ruined cities of Pithom and Raamses support the dates as they do the Biblical account, and it has even been supposed that Raamses—the new residence of Ramses II—was built on the earlier Hyksos capital, Avaris, the Biblical Zoan.

But Seti I's eighteen years' reign and the sixty-six years' dominion of Ramses II are not nearly of so long a duration as the oppression described in the Bible, which lasted four hundred or, according to another account, four hundred and thirty years. This length of time is feasible, however, if we accept the suggestion that Jacob and his sons arrived in the country at the time of the Hyksos invasion. Although no definite date can be given to these occurrences we do know of the Hyksos that, after a slow invasion of the delta region round about 1660 B.C., they obtained dominion over Lower and Middle Egypt and began a century of foreign overlordship.

Moses freed the people from their Egyptian bondage. Who was Moses?

History is fond of veiling the childhood of its heroes in mystery. Moses as a small baby was placed in a rush basket and entrusted to the river and, although the Pharaoh had ordered all new-born male children of the Hebrew to be killed, Moses miraculously survived.

'Hebrews' was then used to describe a low social caste of homeless population elements, people who had come to Egypt and taken service with the Pharaoh or lived there as slaves—a class for whose existence there is also documentary evidence in Mesopotamia and Canaan.

Whereas the stories of the patriarchs, out of a distant and obscure past, are particularly vivid as to the small details of everyday life, the life of Moses, historically much nearer, is replete with miracles. We learn little of his personal life.

Moses grew up at the Egyptian court as the son of the princess who had found him in the water. He killed an Egyptian who was maltreating a Hebrew. Threatened by the Pharaoh, he fled to Midian. The land was given its name by one of the six sons of Abraham and his second wife (or concubine) Keturah; it extended across the desert to the east and south of Canaan; thus the Midianites belonged to Moses' kin. He continued to live with them in the house of the priest Jethro (also known as Raguel), whose daughter, Zipporah, he took to wife; she bore him two sons, Gershom and Eliezer.

His first vision of God on the mountain of Horeb (Sinai) revealed to him the power of God over nature—the burning bush was not consumed. Anxious to discover the cause of the phenomenon, Moses approached the spot. He was warned by a voice '...the place whereon thou standest is holy ground'—and God revealed himself as the God of his fathers, the God of Abraham, of Isaac and of Jacob.

What memories did Moses have of the God of his fathers? What contact did he have with his humbled people? The Bible has this to say:

> And it came to pass in those days, when Moses was grown, that he went out unto his brethren, and looked on their burdens....
> (EXODUS 2, 11)

It was the burden of slavery from which Moses was charged by God to deliver the children of Israel, so as to lead them into the Promised Land. But Moses, who had not shared the fate of his people, asked God his name, for he doubted whether the God of his fathers had remained a reality for his people. And God revealed his name as 'Jahveh': 'I am that I am', the dynamic formula of the always being, always becoming—of the always creating God; the same God who formerly watched over the patriarchs and who, under his new name, took charge of his people's destiny.

There is no written testimony, no documentary evidence outside the Bible for Moses' historical existence. But on the dividing line between legendary obscurity and history, nothing can be explained unless his existence is taken into account: the becoming a people, their religious development and Law, the exodus and the conquest of the land.

THE FIRST RETURN

Moses hesitated to accept the task God assigned to him. 'Who am I, that I should go unto Pharaoh, and that I should bring forth the children of Israel out of Egypt?' Although Moses knew the holy name of God and had received from his God the power of magic signs—indispensable testimony of a divine mission in the ancient world—he tried to evade the task with the excuse: 'I am slow of speech, and of a slow tongue.' And yet who could be more suited to this mission than Moses? By descent he was related to the Hebrews, and both his upbringing at the Egyptian court and his free status put him in a position to deal with the Pharaoh. 'Is not Aaron the Levite thy brother? I know that he can speak well.... And he shall be thy spokesman unto the people, and he shall be, even he shall be, to thee instead of a mouth, and thou shalt be to him instead of God.' Before the people Aaron now spoke the words full of the promise of freedom. 'And the people believed'—thus runs the early (Jahvist) account.

The later (priestly) narrator paints a picture that is probably closer to reality: the children of Israel, broken in body and soul, will not hearken to their liberator. Moses is discouraged: '...how then shall Pharaoh hear me?' Pharaoh, whom Moses wants to deprive of his slaves, refuses to let them go.

> Then the Lord said unto Moses, Now shalt thou see what I will do to Pharaoh; for with a strong hand shall he let them go.... (EXODUS 6, 1)

There followed miracle upon miracle—plagues visited by God upon Egypt. The Nile is turned to blood; frogs, lice, flies, pestilence, boils and blains, hail and locusts beset the land of Egypt, and it is clothed in darkness.

And the Lord said, I have surely seen the affliction of my people which are in Egypt..., and I am come down to deliver them out of the hand of the Egyptians and to bring them up... unto a good land and a large, unto a land flowing with milk and honey.... Come now therefore and I will send thee unto Pharaoh, that thou mayest bring forth my people the Children of Israel out of Egypt.

(EXODUS 3; 7, 8, 10)

And he (God) said, Draw not nigh hither: put off thy shoes from off thy feet, for the place whereon thou standest is holy ground. (EXODUS 3, 5)
Wall-painting from the synagogue of Dura-Europos (c. A.D. 200).

In Moses' time mankind had not yet discarded ideas of primitive magic. Moses' magic staff—just like the mercury wands of the Phoenicians, Arabs and Greeks—was part of the stock-in-trade of religions tainted with magic. But during the exodus and the trek across the desert, Moses' staff served as the highest manifestation of God's intention to support his people in want and danger.

The 'miracles' performed with the help of the staff before the eyes of the people confirmed Moses' divine mission and strengthened the people's trust in the God who had sent him.

AND MIRIAM ANSWERED THEM:

Sing ye to the Lord.
For he hath triumphed
gloriously;
the horse and his rider hath he
thrown into the sea.

(EXODUS 15, 21)

Stretch out thine hand over the sea, that the waters may come again upon the Egyptians....
(EXODUS 14, 26)
Wall-painting in the synagogue at Dura-Europos (*c.* A.D. 200).

The position of the lake 'Red Sea' is not known. Between the lagoon of Serbonis east of the Nile delta (the Egyptian Bardawil) and the sea there is a narrow strip of land that can be traversed in good weather. An escape along this route would tally with the description in the Bible, according to which the children of Israel walked dryshod between the waters. Some scholars believe their crossing place to have been a papyrus swamp in the northern part of the Suez isthmus or one of the lakes through which the Suez canal now runs; others assume the miracle of the sea happened somewhere near the present town of Suez.

CAPTIONS TO COLOUR PLATES

Page 33: Donkeys were the mounts and beasts of burden of the patriarchs. Balaam's ass saw the angel of God and spoke to its master. It was on a donkey that Jesus rode into Jerusalem.

Pages 34/35: The haughty Bedouin ride camels. 'And I will draw water for thy camels also, until they have done drinking', said Rebekah to Abraham's servant, Eliezer.

Page 36: 'As the lily among thorns, so is my love among the daughters.' (Song of Solomon 2, 2)

Of course it is possible to find natural explanations for these miracles. But the Bible did not record them for the purpose of setting scientific problems for posterity. Their significance lies purely and simply in the proof they give of the superiority of Jahveh's power to that of Pharaoh and his gods. Their meaning is found in Moses' cry of triumph: 'Who is like unto thee, O Lord, among the gods?' when the children of Israel had attained their freedom after crossing the Red Sea.

The tenth and worst plague preceded the exodus from Egypt. It was the killing of every first-born of Egypt. 'It is a night to be much observed unto the Lord....' So that the angel of death may 'pass over' the dwellings of Israel, God ordered that their door-posts should be smeared with the blood of a lamb. In haste, and ready for immediate departure, the children of Israel's last meal on Egyptian soil was the flesh of a lamb, with unleavened bread and bitter herbs, the 'bread of affliction' prepared in the 'bitterness' of slavery.

The feast of the Passover, which derives its name from the Hebrew *passaoh,* is held in memory of that night and still celebrates the freeing of the people from Egyptian bondage—the most important event of their history.

The Bible tells how the Pharaoh, broken by the fury of the final plague, let the children of Israel go. But there is also mention of the flight of the people. This latter seems more likely.

How many got away? The number mentioned in the Bible is six hundred thousand able-bodied men, not counting women and children. But the word *eleph* (thousand) also means kinship or family. There were probably a few thousand, and to provide them with food—quails and manna notwithstanding—but especially with water must have been difficult enough, and Moses was repeatedly compelled to pacify the mutinous crowd.

The problem of escaping lay in the avoidance of much-frequented military routes and of the strongly fortified belt in the eastern Nile delta built by Egypt to repel invaders. The usual short overland route to Canaan, anachronistically called 'way of the land of the Philistines' in the Bible, was well guarded. The children of Israel therefore went southwards, reached Succoth (believed to be among the ruins of Tell el Maskhuta) and encamped in Etham, at the edge of the wilderness. The same escape route is described in an Egyptian account of the pursuit of two escaped slaves and the *Hetem* to which it refers might be the Etham of the Bible. But its exact position cannot be ascertained; as with other Biblical references to places, we have only a general idea of their whereabouts. This is particularly true of the 'Red Sea' (actually the Sea of Reeds) which the children of Israel crossed dryshod.

The Bible tells how the waters of the Red Sea, which had divided before the children of Israel, flowed back to engulf the men, horses and chariots of the pursuing Egyptians under the waves. Israel was free.

...When thou hast brought forth the people out of Egypt, ye shall
serve God upon this mountain. (EXODUS 3, 12)

By way of Marah, the place of the miracle of the spring, Elim, with its 'twelve wells of water, and threescore and ten palm trees', and Rephidim where there was a successful battle against the Amalekites (a people living in south of Canaan to the east of the wilderness of Shur), the children of Israel reached their destination in the third month after the exodus.

And Moses went up unto God, and the Lord called unto him out of
the mountain, saying, Thus shalt thou say to the house of Jacob, and
tell the children of Israel; Ye have seen what I did unto the Egyp-

tians, and how I bare you on eagles' wings, and brought you unto myself. Now, therefore, if ye will obey my voice indeed, and keep my covenant, ye shall be a peculiar treasure unto me above all people: for all the earth is mine: And ye shall be unto me a kingdom of priests, and an holy nation. (EXODUS 19, 3–6)

The apparition of God on the mountain, accompanied by the raging of the elements, marks the dramatic climax of the exodus. Moses went alone into 'the thick darkness where God was' while the people, in fear and terror of their lives, waited at a respectful distance for Moses' return. 'And Moses went down unto the people' to whom he proclaimed the Ten Commandments.

Moses, chosen to be the mediator of divine revelation, gives the children of Israel their unconditional Law and in the covenant he has renewed with Jahveh unites the tribes he has led out of Egypt into one entity; for the people are chosen on condition that they keep the covenant. Israel's existence as a people began with an act that was both religious and revolutionary, a unique phenomenon that marked the entry into history of the People of Israel. Thereafter Israel's history was the history of this covenant.

There had been law of usage and legal rescripts, like Hammurabi's law-code already referred to above, long before Moses' time. But Israel's moral commandments, such as the consecration of the seventh day as a day of rest (Sabbath) for man and beast, the right of the poor to glean and to pick fruit from the borders of the fields, the leaving of fields fallow every seventh year and the command to love others, were revolutionary in the culture area of the ancient east. An equally revolutionary law was the obligatory emancipation of slaves in the seventh year.

A quite unprecedented ordinance was that forbidding the making of images of living things or of God. This ordinance was broken while Moses was away on the mountain for forty days and forty nights. In their irresistible desire for visible gods, the multitude made Aaron their instrument, and Aaron fashioned the Golden Calf. Moses, returning from his vigil on the mountain bearing the stone tables of the testimony, broke them in anger at the drunken debauchery of the people as they danced round their idol.

And God again renewed his covenant with the people. Moses was given two more tables, this testimony being put into a precious ark, the 'Ark of the Covenant'—Israel's oldest religious symbol. And when God had appointed the tribe of the Levites to serve as priests and Moses had dedicated his brother Aaron and the latter's sons to the priesthood, the ark was carried by the Levites before the people of Israel during their journey through the desert, and while they rested it was placed in the 'Tent of Reunion', the tabernacle, where Moses met God 'mouth to mouth' and was his mediator with the people. The ark symbolized the presence of God who dwells in heaven and tarries on earth.

Kadesh-Barnea where they 'abode many days' was the last and by far the longest halting place before the conquest of Canaan.

> And the Lord spake unto Moses, saying, Send thou men, that they
> may search the land of Canaan, which I give unto the children of
> Israel: of every tribe of their fathers shall ye send a man, every one a
> ruler among them. (NUMBERS 13, 1–2)

Returning to Kadesh-Barnea, the spies were enthusiastic about the country's fertility, but advised against an attack on its fortified, well-defended towns. Caleb and Joshua alone urged the people to invade Canaan.

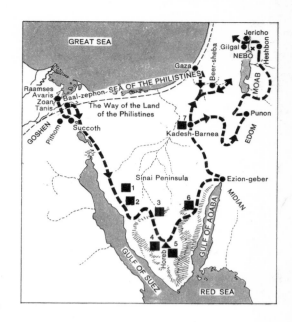

The exodus of the children of Israel out of Egypt and the memorable stages of their desert journey.
1. Marah, the place of the miracle of the spring.
2. '... Elim, where were twelve wells of water, and three score and ten palm trees...'
3. 'And at even the quails came...'
4. '... and pitched at Rephidim...' A victorious battle against the Amalekites.
5. God appears on Mount Horeb (Sinai), the dramatic climax of the exodus. And Moses proclaimed to the children of Israel their binding Law.
6. '... and behold, Miriam became leprous...'
7. Kadesh-Barnea, the last and longest halt before the conquest of Canaan.

And Moses sent them to spy out the land of Canaan, and said unto them, Get you up this way southward, and go up into the mountain: And see the land, what it is: and the people that dwelleth therein, whether they be strong or weak, few or many; and what the land is that they dwell in, whether it be good or bad; and what cities they be that they dwell in, whether in tents or in strong holds; and what the land is, whether it be fat or lean, whether

there be wood therein or not. And be ye of good courage and bring of the fruit of the land. Now the time was the time of the firstripe grapes. (NUMBERS 13, 17–20)
Woodcut from a Haggada (Basle 1816).

THE CONQUEST OF THE LAND

The Bible contains two contradictory accounts of the conquest of the country. The Book of Joshua maintains that the land was conquered in the course of three successive campaigns of Joshua, while the first chapter of Judges implies a gradual infiltration by the tribes into regions that had been allotted to them, the conquest and defence of which was largely their own affair. It is difficult, even with our present knowledge, to reconstruct the historical course of events from the Biblical account, much revised by later Jewish historiographers, in which Moses and Joshua occupy the centre of the stage. Yet Joshua's strategy seems altogether plausible.

'The princes are prostrate and cry "Mercy!"
Not one lifts his head among the Nine Bows.
Libya is destroyed, the land of the Hittites
is pacified,
Canaan plundered with every ill.
Ashkelon is taken, Gezer seized
Jenoam made as though it had never been,
Israel is laid waste and hath no seed,
Palestine is become a widow for Egypt'.

From the granite victory stele of Pharaoh Merenptah (1224–1214 B.C.).

Canaan, for the conquest of which the tribes of Israel were arming, had experienced in the stormy course of her history a long series of migrations and invasions which had inhibited the establishment of a lasting and unified political structure. During the second half of the second millennium B.C. control of Canaan can be seen as maintaining the balance of power in the struggle between the great rulers of the Near East.

The Amurru (Amorites), who gradually became assimilated with the already existing population, made little impact on the dominant influence of Egypt in Canaan. Egyptian rule suffered no interruption until the Hyksos era (c. 1660–1550 B.C.). An illuminating comment in the Bible (Numbers 13, 22) tells us that Hebron was built seven years before Zoan, the Hyksos capital in the Nile delta. Although there are no immediate sources in respect of this period, it may be assumed that the arrival of the Hyksos represented the culmination of vast population movements in the north, and that they first occupied Canaan before they invaded Egypt. The remains of strong fortifications such as glacis and moats belonging to this time have been found in many Canaanite towns such as Lachish, Megiddo, Beth-shan, Ashkelon, Jaffa and Gezer, and it is possible that the vast walled enclosures found in some towns such as Hazor may have been used to store horse-drawn chariots—a new method of warfare to which the Hyksos owed their victories. Hyksos rule, which proved humiliating for Egypt, brought Canaan and its inhabitants to their highest flowering.

After the Hyksos had been expelled by the Pharaoh Aahmose in about 1550 B.C., Egypt regained supremacy over the region of Canaan. The country deteriorated, becoming a mere object of exploitation for the Egyptians who were interested above all in her ports, the security of the caravan routes and in tribute. There were uprisings. Under the leadership of the prince of Kadesh on the Orontes, the Canaanite city-states united to form a comprehensive coalition. Tuthmosis III (1490–1436) was the first to succeed in breaking up the alliance of the towns when he conquered Megiddo in 1468 and after numerous campaigns went on to consolidate Egyptian power by means of strict military and economic administration.

In 1375 B.C. the Hittites had only just finished dealing a death-blow to the Mittannian kingdom, weakened by internal confusion, when they took the latter's place in the bitter contest with Egypt for supremacy over Canaan.

But Egypt was then shaken to her foundations by a religious movement and this was to prove fatal to her hegemony in the Near East. Under Amenhotep III (1400–1378) and to an even greater extent under his successor, Amenhotep IV (Akhenaten), Egypt's supremacy in Canaan was seriously endangered. This is evident from the state of continuous warfare and local skirmishes depicted in the Amarna tablets we have already mentioned. These also speak of the *Apiru*, a word related to the appellation *Hebrews*, meaning here those semi-nomadic tribes which roved between the city-states. The existence of Apiru in Canaan in the fourteenth century would seem to show that not all the tribes accompanied Jacob when he went to Egypt.

It was mainly under the Pharaohs Seti I and Ramses II that Egypt succeeded in reasserting her overlordship in Canaan, though not over the northern part of the country. Egypt's struggle with the Hittite kingdom was at its height, but the two powers reached an agreement in 1269 B.C. when they established a frontier between their respective spheres of interest; this was the northern frontier of the Land of Canaan, as it is described in the Bible (Numbers 34).

This development brought about both the rise of the kingdoms of Edom, Moab and Ammon east of the Jordan, and also the invasion of nomads and semi-nomads from the east. Since these kingdoms, with which Israel negotiated for safe passage, were set up round about the beginning of the thirteenth century B.C., the conquest of the country can be assumed to have taken place during the second half of the thirteenth century.

The first assault broke on the well-fortified line of defence which commanded access from the south. Israel was beaten by the king of Arad at Hormah. But the first decisive victory was not long in coming. The Israelites skirted Edom and Moab to the east, having been refused transit through their territories, they then crossed the River Arnon, vanquished the Amorite king Sihon, near Jahaz, and King Og of Bashan near Edrei, and in this way Gilead in East Jordan fell into their hands.

Moses' time was fulfilled. He did not live to experience what followed. He saw the Promised Land from Mount Nebo and, as legend has it, God kissed him and he died. His final resting-place is not known.

Joshua took on the leadership. After the memorable crossing of the Jordan, the children of Israel celebrated their first feast of the Passover in the Holy Land, at their headquarters at Gilgal. They were outside Jericho.

The ancient city fell. Ai, too, was razed to the ground after the inhabitants had been tricked into an ambush. But Joshua's attack was in fact unlikely to have been upon Ai, which was then uninhabited, but rather against nearby Beth-el, which does have a burnt level dating back to the thirteenth century B.C.

The fame of Joshua and of his powerful God spread like wildfire. But the Canaanites rose 'to fight with Joshua and with Israel with one accord'. Only the Gibeonites fraudulently made a pact with Israel, by pretending that they came from a far country. Joshua, believing them to be harmless, agreed. But an alliance of five Canaanite kings marched against the renegade Gibeonites, and there was a battle.

> ...Sun, stand thou still upon Gibeon; and thou, Moon, in the valley of Ajalon. And the sun stood still, and the moon stayed, until the people had avenged themselves on their enemies. (JOS. 10, 12–13)

After this, the cities of Makkedah, Libnah, Lachish and Eglon in the western highlands, as also Hebron and Debir, were captured. Finally, in his third campaign, Joshua pressed northwards and destroyed Hazor in Galilee. The destruction levels in these towns show that a major invasion took place in the second half of the thirteenth century. One of the towns that did not fall was Sichem whose population, it may be supposed, consisted largely of Hebrew elements, aware of their kinship with the Israelites.

An inscription of 1219 B.C. on the famous stele of the Pharaoh Merenptah (son and successor of Ramses II) is the first written record other than the Bible to mention the name of Israel, referring to her as one of the 'foreign peoples' to have been conquered by Egypt. This victory has not been historically confirmed, but the inscription proves

And when the inhabitants of Gibeon
heard what Joshua had done
unto Jericho and to Ai,
they did work wilily, and went and
made,
as if they had been ambassadors,
and took old sacks upon their asses,
and wine bottles, old, and rent,
and bound up; and old shoes
and clouted upon their feet,
and old garments upon them;
and all the bread of their provision
was dry and mouldy.
And they went to Joshua unto the camp
at Gilgal, and said unto him,
and to the men of Israel,
We be come from a far country:
now therefore make ye a league with us.

(JOSHUA 9, 3–6)

The Bible gives an impressive description of how the walls of the ancient city of Jericho fell without a single blow being struck when warriors, followed by priests bearing the ark, marched seven times round the town to the sound of trumpets. Archaeology regards the account with scepticism, since no trace has been found of the walls of this town, so often destroyed in the course of its history of several thousand years. It is assumed that Jericho was abandoned in the fourteenth century B.C.

Woodcut from a Haggada (1629).

The inhabitants
of the villages ceased,
they ceased in Israel,
until that I Deborah arose,
that I arose a mother in Israel.
... was there a shield or spear
seen among forty thousand
in Israel?...
Awake, awake Deborah:
awake, awake, utter a song:
arise, Barak,
and lead thy captivity captive,
thou son of Abinoam.
Then he made him
that remaineth
have dominion over the nobles
among the people:
the Lord made me have
dominion over the mighty.
... And the princes of Issachar
were with Deborah...
For the divisions of Reuben
there were great searchings
of heart....
Zebulun and Naphtali
were a people
that jeoparded their lives
unto the death
in the high places
of the field.
The kings came and fought,
then fought the kings of Canaan
in Taanach
by the waters of Megiddo:
they took no gain of money.
They fought from heaven;
the stars in their courses
fought against Sisera.

(JUDGES 5; 7, 8, ·12, 13, 15, 18–20)

Its archaic style shows the song of Deborah
to be contemporaneous; it is the earliest Israelite epos handed down to us through the Bible
(about 1125 B.C.).

that there was a people of Israel at this time in Canaan. The Israelites no doubt were living in the country but had not finally settled there; their conquests and their new habitats were probably confined to mountainous areas, and it was only gradually that they were able to advance into the fertile coastal plains. Research has shown that the conquest of the land was a long painful process and that it was only with the time of the Kings that the tribes achieved stability and definite frontiers.

THE TIME OF THE JUDGES

During the period of about 150 years which preceded the kingdom, Israel was a cult community made up of twelve tribes united by their covenant with Jahve. Each member of the covenant was bound to give military aid to any tribe that was threatened, and all were responsible for the safety of a central sanctuary containing the Ark of the Covenant which eventually became established at Shiloh.

For the first time in their history their desire to settle compelled the tribes to seek a relationship which was not merely transitory with the existing populations in Canaan, either by fighting them or by coming to terms with them. These encounters, which often led to the worship of local deities, brought about a recurring pattern of apostasy and reconversion. Apostasy from God was followed by defeat, repentance brought victory—the gift of Jahveh.

But the process of coming to terms with a culturally superior population and the gradual transition, during the time of the Judges, from a nomadic to a sedentary condition weakened the tribal way of life, dissipated their strength, and even led to rivalry between tribes, the northern and southern ones in particular. There was absolutely no planned, organized power. Only at moments of pressing danger would several tribes temporarily combine for common action: the God of Israel saved his people through those whom he raised up, the 'Judges'. Divine inspiration, therefore, invested these leaders with authority in their struggle against neighbouring peoples. When Abimelech, son of the judge Gideon, sought to inherit his father's privileged position and set up a kingdom in Sichem by force, his end was equally violent.

The first three Judges were followed by the prophetess Deborah. It was in her time that the decisive battle took place between Israel and the Canaanites. On the enemy side there was Sisera, the military commander of King Jabin of Hazor, with a strong force of charioteers; he was opposed by Deborah's commander, Barak, with warriors from six tribes. Barak's army was inspired by Deborah, and the battle ended in victory at Megiddo by the River Kishon.

Israel's triumph strengthened her desire for a national existence and national power. But another consequence was the widespread invasion of cultivated land by desert nomads with, at the forefront, the camel-borne Midianites. Gideon, the judge, opposed them. At God's command, he destroyed the altar of Baal at Ophrah. After this, with only a small number of select warriors, he vanquished the dreaded opponent. Offered the crown by his grateful people, he refused.

Jephthah, the judge from Gilead, a masterly diplomat and excellent general, saved the country from the Ammonites who had attempted to retake the territory captured by Israel at the beginning of her conquests. Determined to abide by his oath to sacrifice to God the first living being he encountered on his return, if victory was vouchsafed him, he saw his daughter come running joyfully to meet him, his only child.

Although the authority of these judge-saviour figures was not hereditary and although they ruled only part of the country, it was through them and through the Jahveh war that Israel developed from a confederation of tribes, in which religion had been the formative and motive power, into a strong military and political people under a central leader. This was not yet, however. For the struggle against the Philistines threatened to end in disaster.

ON THE TRACK OF THE PHILISTINES

The Philistines were one of the sea-peoples whose barbarian invasions, continuing from the late thirteenth century onwards, had transformed the Near East. North Canaan and, with few exceptions, the coastal towns from Ugarit to Ashkelon fell victim to their murderous raids and attacks.

Their assault on Egypt failed, however. Ramses III (1198–1167 B.C.) succeeded in driving them off the coast of the Nile delta, and also halted their advance in a memorable land battle. The persistent aggression of the Philistines was thus turned back against south Canaan and soon (about 1175) they had achieved uncontested dominion over Ashkelon, now rebuilt, over Ashdod and Gaza, over Ekron and Gath. Their knowledge of iron and how to work it, probably derived from the Hittites, gave them superiority in war. The final decline of Egyptian power in Canaan had become irreversible, and Philistine settlement was all the more menacing for Israel. The tribe of Dan was particularly exposed to Philistine expansion. It was a Danite, Samson, who became the hero of the folk legend which illuminates the beginning of the Israel-Philistine struggle. The peculiar fabric of adventure, humour, love, betrayal and real greatness which lends charm to the Bible story of Samson, completely masks the genuine historical basis of this unusual figure from Judges. The tribe of Dan, unable any longer to hold their territory against their hostile neighbour, migrated northwards to a new and distant habitat at the sources of the Jordan.

The Philistines now commanded the whole of the lowlands along the south-west coast of Canaan, and were making preparations for the conquest of the mountainous central area of Ephraim and Benjamin. There was a battle at Aphek (1 Sam. 4). At the very first encounter the Israelites succumbed to the crushingly superior forces of the enemy. As an act of desperation, they had the Ark of the Covenant brought from Shiloh to their military headquarters, and, filled with holy enthusiasm, they once more hurled themselves against the foe. But the catastrophic defeat of Israel was to teach the people a hard lesson. The ark fell into the hands of the Philistines. The judgement with which Hophni and Phinehas, sons of the priest Eli, had been threatened was fulfilled when they were killed in battle. Eli died when he heard of the loss of the ark. Shiloh was burnt to the ground. And for several decades the Philistines were Egypt's successors in western Jordan.

Although the Philistines returned their ill-omened booty at the earliest opportunity, accompanying it with gifts of atonement, the confidence of the people in their priests could not be restored; it had already been undermined by the greed and immorality of Hophni and Phinehas when they had been of priests at Shiloh. At a time of grave crisis, when their whole existence was threatened, the people looked to a unifying power such as other peoples possessed. They demanded a king.

Habitat of the twelve tribes of Israel at the time of Judges.

'... and he (Samson) judged Israel twenty years.' (JUDGES 16, 31) This remark would seem to be a later addition to the 'Jahvist' text concerned solely with a popular hero endowed by God with Herculean strength. He mocks the Philistines by lifting the heavy gate of the city off its hinges and carrying it away. With the jawbone of an ass he slays a thousand of his enemies. But he succumbs to the wiles of a woman, Delilah, to whom he betrays the secret of his strength—as a Nazarite dedicated to God, he must not shave the hair of his head. Delilah's treachery delivered him up to the vengeance of

the Philistines, who blinded him. Exposed to the derision of the people as they were merry-making, he called upon God, who gave him back his strength. He broke the pillars of the temple in which the revellers were assembled, burying himself and his enemies among the rubble.

Floor mosaic in St. Gereon's Church, Cologne (twelfth century).

THE TIME OF THE KINGS

THE TRAGIC FIGURE OF SAUL

And Samuel... said,
This will be the manner
of the king
that shall reign over you:
He will take your sons,
and appoint them
for himself,
for his chariots
and to be his horsemen;
and some shall
run before his chariots...
And he will take your fields,
and your vineyards,
and your oliveyards,
even the best of them,
and give them
to his servants.
And he will take
the tenth of your seed,
and of your vineyards,
and give to his officers
and to his servants.
...He will take
the tenth of your sheep:
and ye shall be his servants.

(I SAMUEL 8; 10, 11, 14, 15–17)

Saul lived a simple country life even when, from the plough, he had risen to the throne. The remains of his citadel at Gibeah, excavated in this century, reveal the modest extent of its fortifications and a complete absence of pomp. His regal powers were equally modest—he had no standing army, no large bodyguard and was largely dependent on the voluntary support of the tribes.

The story of Saul, son of Kish of the tribe of Benjamin, begins in the Bible like a fairy-tale. Searching for strayed asses, he asks the advice of the 'seer' Samuel. And Samuel receives him as the chosen king of God.

In Samuel, priest, prophet and last judge of Israel, there had arisen a man whose passionate nature and steady activity succeeded in building up the religious and spiritual resilience of his people in spite of Philistine supremacy. Samuel upheld the sole kingship of God; and he feared to see his own power curtailed by a worldly ruler. In his speech on the 'law of the king' he warns the people of impending tributes, forced labour and expropriation. Yet the people insist. They want a king to arbitrate and to lead them in war.

And when the clouds began to gather over East Jordan as well, the hour of the people had come. The Ammonite king Nahash besieged Jabesh in Gilead, and the beleaguered in their desperation were prepared to surrender. He countered with the insolent demand that every citizen in the town should have his right eye put out, and was asked for a respite. The town sent messengers to Gibeah, and Saul, who had just come 'after the herd out of the field', was told of the shameful peace terms.

> And the spirit of God came upon Saul, ...and his anger was kindled greatly. And he took a yoke of oxen, and hewed them in pieces, and sent them throughout all the coasts of Israel by the hands of messengers, saying, Whosoever cometh not forth after Saul and after Samuel, so shall it be done unto his oxen. And the fear of the Lord fell on the people, and they came out with one consent. (I SAM. 11, 6–7)

In their exuberance over the victorious battle near Jabesh which established Saul's military fame, the people demanded the death of Saul's opponents and elected their leader king in Gilgal—one of the most pregnant decisions of Israel's history. The people had their king. But royal power was bound to have far-reaching effects upon the existing tribal way of life and to lead to conflicts with religious tradition.

Samuel laid down the office of judge. And although he anointed Saul, the prophet's hostile attitude towards the king was plainly evident. Samuel's urgent exhortation to the people culminates in bitter reproaches for their having wanted a king.

Saul, who excelled all his people in beauty and stature, was to the last a tolerant and righteous king and a great military leader. It was this latter quality that counted for most with the people, who desired freedom from the yoke of the Philistines. It was plain that the latter were not prepared for Saul's victorious resistance supported by his people's overwhelming desire for freedom. Their unsuspecting garrison in Gibeah was surprised by Jonathan, the son of Saul, in a swift attack. That meant war. The Philistines gathered at Michmash, north-east of Gibeah, with 'six thousand horsemen, and people as the sand which is on the seashore in multitude': To oppose them, Saul had only an ill-equipped people's army.

During the campaign there was a heated exchange between Saul and Samuel who had promised the king to offer up a sacrifice before the battle. Saul waited seven days for him in Gilgal but in vain. It was only when the warriors started to desert him that Saul offered up the sacrifice himself. Then Samuel appeared, reproached Saul for his disobedience, declared his kingdom would not survive, and that God had already chosen one who was more worthy.

Deprived of divine support, Saul's kingship was without substance. His downfall was already foreshadowed.

But Israel, almost completely surrounded by the Philistines, was in mortal danger. Then the impossible happened. Accompanied only by his armour-bearer, who 'slew after him', Jonathan rushed in among the Philistine army which he threw into complete confusion, and Israel smote the enemy from 'Michmash to Ajalon'. But the issue had not yet been decided.

A little later, after a battle against the Amalekites in the south—it was to be Saul's last victory—the final breach took place between Samuel and the king. Samuel returned to his home town of Ramah and Saul to Gibeah. They never saw each other again. But Samuel set out to find the new king.

Samuel anoints David king. 'Then Samuel took the horn of oil and anointed him in the midst of his brethren....' (I SAMUEL 16, 13)
Wall-painting from the Dura-Europos Synagogue (c. A.D. 200).

DAVID—SHEPHERD, SINGER, HERO AND KING

David, the youngest son of Jesse, was still a boy who looked after the sheep when Samuel arrived at his birthplace, Bethlehem.

> Then Samuel took the horn of oil, and anointed him in the midst of his brethren: and the Spirit of the Lord came upon David from that day forward... But the Spirit of the Lord departed from Saul...
> (I SAM. 16, 13–14)

Saul's royal dignity had been impaired; he had come to grief because of conflict between the demands of the throne and those of the priesthood, and, victim of the lack of definition obtaining between those two spheres, the tension was too much for him. His emotions were poisoned by suspicion, and he was tormented by delusions.

So David, a youth of radiant beauty, was summoned to the court to soothe the melancholy king with his harp-playing. The Bible tells how Saul came to love David.

The Philistines made good use of Israel's internal dissensions, increased their fighting strength and prepared to strike back at Azekah, at the foot of the Judean mountains. Only the valley of Elah lay between them and the forces of Saul. Day after day the Philistine Goliath advanced from their ranks, a man of enormous stature, bristling with weapons, and mockingly suggested settlement by single combat, when the people of the vanquished submit to the people of the victor.

No one wanted to take on the unequal fight, although Saul had promised his daughter's hand to the victor. But David, used to protecting his herds against wild animals with a sling, and with the daredevil courage of youth, went out fearlessly to meet Goliath. With unerring aim he hit him in the forehead and killed the fallen giant with his own sword. Once again the arch-enemy had been brought to his knees.

But the Lord said unto Samuel,
Look not on his countenance,
or on the height of his stature...
for the Lord seeth not
as man seeth;
for man looketh on the outward appearance,
but the Lord looketh on the heart....
Again, Jesse
made seven of his sons
to pass before Samuel.
And Samuel said unto Jesse,
The Lord hath not chosen these...
Are here all thy children?
And he (Jesse) said,
There remaineth yet the youngest,
and behold, he keepeth the sheep...
And he sent, and brought him in...
And the Lord said,
Arise, anoint him;
for this is he.

(I SAMUEL 16; 7, 10–12)

Historically speaking, it is unlikely that David was anointed during the lifetime of Saul.

The Lord is my shepherd
I shall not want.
He maketh me to lie down
in green pastures:
He leadeth me beside
the still waters.
He restoreth my soul:
He leadeth me in the paths
of righteousness
for his name's sake.
Yea, though I walk through
the valley of the shadow
of death,
I will fear no evil:
for thou art with me,
thy rod and thy staff
they comfort me.
Thou preparest a table
before me
in the presence of mine enemies:
thou anointest my head with oil;
my cup runneth over.
Surely goodness and mercy
shall follow me
all the days of my life:
and I will dwell in
the house of the Lord for ever.

(THE GOOD SHEPHERD, PSALM 23)

CAPTIONS TO COLOUR PLATES

Page 45: The Negev Desert has a changeable face.

Page 46: The Plain of Jezreel, with the Mountains of Gilboa in the background. It was there that King Saul and his sons fell in battle against the Philistines.

Page 47: Lumps of salt by the Dead Sea.

Page 48: Rocky landscape by the Dead Sea. In these gorges David hid from Saul.

Saul made the young hero a commander in his army. David conquered all hearts. But there was a song that ran 'Saul hath slain his thousands, and David his ten thousands', which aroused the king's jealousy. In the hope of getting rid of David by sending him on a dangerous mission, Saul demanded that he should kill a hundred Philistines by way of a marriage gift to his daughter. David killed two hundred. He was given Michal in marriage, but Saul had become his bitter enemy. The close friendship between David and Saul's son Jonathan saved him from the king's murderous intentions. David fled—alone, unarmed and without provisions.

He took refuge with the priests of Nob, near Gibeah. They gave him some of the shewbread from the sanctuary, and the Goliath's sword which they had kept. The priests were betrayed to the king, an appalling bloodbath ensued, and only one of them, Abiathar, escaped. This man, a son of the priest Ahimelech, fought his way out and went to join David as his companion in exile.

David was an outlaw. After being with Achish, king of Gath, he fled to Abdullam, a district of many caves, where he remained in hiding. His brothers and parents joined him. Soon a band of several hundred people had gathered round him, malcontents, debtors and down-and-outs.

As commander of this band of freebooters, David freed the town of Keilah from the Philistines, but failed to find protection within its gates from Saul, who set out to capture him. Moving restlessly from place to place among the wild mountains of Judea, he came to the wilderness of Ziph, where his friend Jonathan came to him at Horeshah.

> ...And he said unto him, Fear not: for the hand of Saul my father shall not find thee; and thou shalt be king over Israel, and I shall be next unto thee; and that also Saul my father knoweth. (I SAM. 23, 17)

Betrayed to Saul, David escaped to the desert of Maon. The king, at the head of a large army, was already on his heels when a Philistine attack forced him hurriedly to turn back. David reached En-gedi.

David and his men eked out a meagre existence in the desert. They protected the servants of great landowners when they were out working and in return asked food of their masters. But one rich man, Nabal of Carmel, roughly turned David's messengers away. Outraged by the shameful treatment of the people who had protected her husband's herds against raiders, Abigail went out to meet David without her husband's knowledge, and gave him all and more than he had asked for. Nabal fell dead—out of fear of David's revenge and rage at the loss of his property. The woman who had acted thus became David's wife.

Twice, during this obsessive pursuit, Saul found himself defenceless and at David's mercy. On both occasions David generously spared his enemy's life; he did not want to lay hand upon 'the anointed of the Lord'. In order to escape once and for all from Saul and his myrmidons, he made a momentous decision: he offered his services and those of his men to the Philistine king Achish, from whom he had once escaped. Achish accorded them asylum, and gave David the town of Ziklag as fief in return for military service. By cleverly manœuvring, David not only succeeded in concealing from the Philistines that many of his campaigns were directed against the dangerous Amalekite attacks on Israel, but also established bonds of friendship with the grateful tribes of the south. The Philistines only once feared betrayal, and on that occasion Achish relieved David of the conflict between vassalage and patriotism by not allowing him to take part in the renewed struggle with Israel.

The Philistines marched from Aphek into the plain of Jezreel, thus driving a wedge between the northern and southern tribes, allied themselves with the Canaanites who

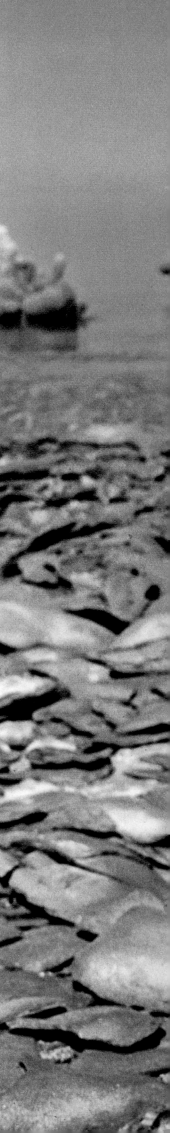

were still overlords in this region and able to make use of their chariots on the level ground; they also held the valuable bases of Beth-shean and Megiddo. In an almost hopeless situation Saul rallied his meagre forces on the slopes of Mount Gilboa so as to prevent the enemy gaining access to the interior through the passes.

But it was too late for any real resistance. The tragedy of Saul drew to a close. He knew he had been abandoned by Jahveh—God 'answered him not that day'. In his need he went to a woman in Endor who was able to conjure up the dead, and asked her to invoke the spirit of Samuel. From the lips of the prophet Saul heard words of doom and the ominous announcement: 'Tomorrow shalt thou and thy sons be with me'.

The Battle of Gilboa (c. 1000 B.C.) ended in an annihilating defeat for Israel. Jonathan and his brothers were killed. Saul fell upon his sword. The people were on the brink of disaster.

At this point David acted. After uttering a heartfelt lament on Saul and Jonathan, he left Ziklag. With a strong following, he entered Hebron and was at once proclaimed by the Judeans and other tribes of the south 'King over the House of Judah' while Ish-bosheth, the only surviving son of Saul, was crowned King of Israel by Saul's general, Abner, at Mahanaim, east of Jordan. For years the land was torn by ferocious civil war. Only after the murder of Ish-bosheth by two of his own captains was the issue decided—all the tribes acclaimed David in Hebron as 'King over all Israel and Judah'.

David perceived clearly where the weakness of the new political set-up lay; it was in the position of Hebron, the natural centre of the land of Judah. With great perspicacity, he settled the question of inter-tribal rivalry by choosing for his residence a city which did not belong to any of the tribes. The city was Jerusalem, an enclave between the two regions and inhabited by Jebusites. Jerusalem fell to David and his trusted followers and became David's city in the truest sense of the word. Twice the Philistines, as allies of the Jebusites, tried to recapture Jerusalem. They were finally defeated by the application of their own tactical methods of warfare—and this act of David's was of fundamental significance in determining the course of history. The sovereign territory of the Philistines was now confined to their cities on the coast: Gaza, Ashkelon, Ashdod, Ekron and Gath. Israel could breathe at last.

David turned eastwards, consolidating his hold over the tribes there and extending his power to the kingdoms of Moab, Ammon and Edom. His biggest triumph, however, was his victory in the north-east over King Hadadezer of Aram-Zobah, who had called in the Ammonites to help him. This part of the Aramean dominion (north-east Jordan), together with Damascus and the caravan routes, became a province of David's state. There is a certain irony in the fact that David's victory over the Arameans freed their neighbour, Assyria, of a dangerous enemy and thus contributed to her rise, which was to have such grave consequences for Israel later on.

David now ruled a major kingdom extending from the Mediterranean to the Syrian desert and from Hamath on the Orontes to the Red Sea. For the first time in history this area, which to the great powers of the Near East had represented a transit-area or a sphere of influence, had become a political entity—a process facilitated by the temporary weakness of the large neighbouring powers. The country was at peace. More or less dependent peoples paid tribute, and thus laid the foundation for Israel's increasing economic prosperity.

Equally capable in civil as in military government, David was circumspect in his choice of officials to administer the state; Joshaphat as 'chancellor', Joab as general, Benaiah as captain of the bodyguard, Abiathar and Zadok as High Priests. And when

DAVID SANG HIS MOVING LAMENT

The beauty of Israel
is slain upon thy high places:
How are the mighty
fallen!
...Ye mountains of Gilboa,
let there be no dew,
neither let there be rain,
upon you,
nor fields of offerings:
for there
the shield of the mighty
is vilely cast away,
the shield of Saul,
as though he had not been
anointed with oil.
...Saul and Jonathan
were lovely and pleasant
in their lives,
and in their death
they were not divided:
they were swifter than eagles,
they were stronger than lions.
I am distressed for thee,
my brother Jonathan:
very pleasant hast thou been
unto me:
thy love to me was wonderful,
passing the love
of women.
How are the mighty fallen,
and the weapons of war
perished!

(II SAMUEL I; 19, 21, 23, 26, 27)

According to the second of the Bible accounts—II SAM. I, 2–16—Saul did not die by his own hand, but was killed by a young Amalekite who took his crown and bracelet to David, hoping for a reward. But David, outraged at the murder of the Lord's anointed, had the Amalekite put to death.

49

And it came to pass in an eveningtide, that David arose from off his bed, and walked upon the roof of the king's house: and from the roof he saw a woman washing herself: and the woman was very beautiful to look upon. And David sent and enquired after the woman. And one said, Is not this Bath-sheba, the daughter of Eliam, the wife of Uriah the Hittite? And David sent messengers and took her....
(II SAMUEL 11, 2–4)

Woodcut by Johann Grüninger (1485).

the king had brought the ark to Jerusalem, the city became the secular and religious centre of the country. By uniting the religious authority of the priesthood with the court while at the same time always knowing when he must defer to it, he succeeded in establishing an unprecedented balance between priesthood and monarchy, though he continued systematically to expand his royal power. It was the dawn of a golden age.

A man of bewitching charm, hero, singer and poet, David was a king after 'God's heart'. Yet even he failed to resist the temptation to act shamefully. Carried away by passion for Bath-sheba, the beautiful wife of Uriah the Hittite, he sent her husband to certain death in a murderous battle, and took Bath-sheba to be his wife.

As though fate were seeking its revenge, his later life was troubled by terrible family strife. Amnon, lusting after his half-sister Tamar, violated her and was killed by her brother Absalom in revenge. David banished Absalom. Even after a conciliatory gesture from his father, Absalom rebelled, having himself proclaimed king in Hebron. David took refuge in Mahanaim. Certain of victory, Absalom returned to Jerusalem and to seal his succession, took over his father's harem. But given deliberately misleading advice by David's devoted friend, Hushai, the rebel delayed his pursuit of the king, thus giving David time to build up his army. During the decisive encounter in a wood which 'devoured more people that day than the sword devoured', Absalom was lifted out of his saddle by a forked branch and was killed by Joab, David's captain. David, who had ordered that his son's life be spared, never forgave Joab. Deeply mourning for Absalom, he returned to Jerusalem.

ISRAEL AT THE HEIGHT OF HER POWER

SOLOMON—SAGE AND DESPOT

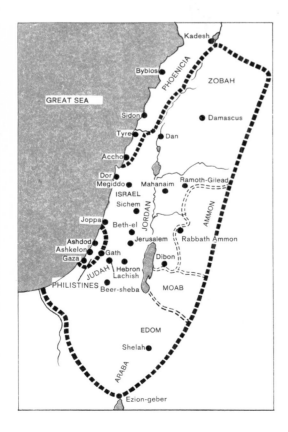

The united kingdom at the time of David.

Solomon, son of David and Bath-sheba, was chosen by his father as his successor, overriding the claims of the elder son, Adonijah. His coronation was preceded by a matter of hours by the seditious attempt of Joab and the priest Abiathar to set up Adonijah as king. Their secret coronation feast at En-Rogel near Jerusalem was barely over when the news reached them that Solomon had been anointed king by Nathan the prophet and the priest Zadok at the well of Gihon. The conspirators fled. Solomon became David's co-regent (c. 961 B.C.).

After David's death, the young king settled accounts with his enemies. Joab was murdered, Abiathar, because he had shared David's exile, was merely banished. But he had Adonijah killed because the latter's request for the hand of the young Abishag, who had lovingly tended David in his old age, aroused his suspicion.

David had left Solomon heir to the most powerful state between Egypt and Assyria. Solomon was king over Israel and Judah and king of Ammon, Moab was ruled by a subject prince; the province of Aram and Edom, which had also been declared a province, were administered by his governors, and both were subject, like the cities of the Philistines, to payment of tribute. But during his forty years' reign, Solomon never tried to increase his dominions, either by warlike or peaceful means, and did not even put down quite considerable uprisings in subject territories.

The Bible tells how, at Gibeon, God appeared in a dream to Solomon who asked him for 'understanding to discern judgment', and how, to this gift, God added those of 'riches and honour'. Tradition ascribes the two books Proverbs and Ecclesiastes to Solomon, the philosopher; he is the father of Hebrew Wisdom Literature. Under Solomon, the trader and diplomat, the land experienced its economic heyday.

Solomon's kingdom possessed immediate access to the Mediterranean at Joppa (Jaffa) and to the Red Sea in the Gulf of Eilat (Aqaba). The caravan routes between Egypt and Mesopotamia traversed his dominions. The domestication of the camel meant that goods could be carried across desert and steppe. Further, the much exploited copper deposits in Arabah and Ezion-geber (at the north end of the Red Sea) were a valuable source of a product much in demand.

Hiram, king of Tyre, had a mutually advantageous trade agreement with Solomon. King Hiram provided both the timber and the experienced craftsmen and seamen; King Solomon built ships, provided oarsmen and sent supplies of grain and oil to the Phoenicians. Laden with copper, Solomon's ships sailed from Ezion-geber to the distant, legendary country of Ophir, returning three years later with gold, balsam, spices and precious stones. Solomon also conducted an *entrepôt* trade, delivering chariots from Egypt to Asia Minor in exchange for the strong Cilician war horses.

Solomon's riches increased. Trade profits, tribute money and revenue from the control of the caravan routes gave rise to building operations of all kinds—garrison and storage towns were built, palaces arose in Jerusalem as a sign of regal magnificence, and upon the royal city the Temple was bestowed.

And Solomon made affinity with Pharaoh king of Egypt, and took Pharaoh's daughter and brought her into the city of David....
(I KINGS 3, 1)
Painted limestone (fourteenth century B.C.).

The common people, however, paid a heavy price for Solomon's building, his extravagant household, and for the army equipped with chariots and kept constantly ready for defence. They were oppressed by the burden of taxation, payment in kind and forced labour. A centralized fiscal and administrative system secured for the monarch revenue, supplies and man-power. 'Israel'—not the Southern Kingdom of Judah which was doubtless also subject to taxation—was divided into twelve administrative districts under governors, and each tax area had to provide for the royal court and government during one month of the year. Class differences made their appearance to exacerbate the distress of the people of Jahveh.

But the fame of Solomon drew visitors from other countries, and crowned heads such as the Queen of Sheba sought his friendship. His marriages with women of standing from neighbouring countries—Solomon's favourite wife was an Egyptian princess—increased the kingdom's repute, and the style of living at court betrayed the splendour-loving oriental potentate. Solomon's wives possessed luxurious houses with their own sanctuaries where they could worship the gods of their country. Foreign cults adulterated the purity of the Jahveh creed, and Solomon himself submitted to their influence.

THE SONG OF SONGS

My beloved spake,
and said unto me,
Rise up, my love,
my fair one,
and come away.
For lo, the winter
is past,
the rain is over
and gone;
The flowers appear
on the earth;
the time of the singing
of birds is come,
and the voice of the turtle
is heard in our land;
the fig tree putteth forth
her green figs,
and the vines
with the tender grape
give a good smell.
Arise, my love, my fair one,
and come away.
O my dove,
that art in the clefts
of the rock,
in the secret places
of the stairs,
let me see thy countenance,
let me hear thy voice;
for sweet is thy voice,
and thy countenance
is comely.

(SONG OF SOLOMON 2, 10–14)

The love song attributed to Solomon, was regarded by the Jews as the expression of God's love for his people, a view that may explain its inclusion in the Bible. Christians interpreted the song as the expression of Jesus' love for the Church.

Like the dwellings of the nomad people—the children of Israel—the 'dwelling' of their God was a tent. 'And thou shalt make curtains of goats' hair to be a covering upon the tabernacle: eleven curtains shalt thou make.'
(EXODUS 26, 7)

Reconstruction of the tabernacle (c. 1600).

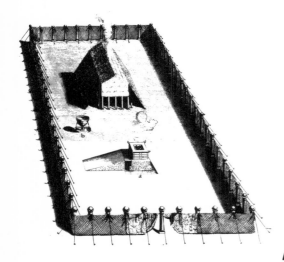

The ark had had a chequered career before being brought by David to Jerusalem. After the miraculous crossing of the River Jordan which was stayed in its course before the ark, the latter was kept in Joshua's headquarters at Gilgal and then at Beth-el, later being taken to Shiloh. In the Battle near Aphek it was seized by the Philistines who placed it in their sanctuary at Ashdod, where it twice caused the figure of their god Dagon to fall to the ground. Returned hastily to Israelite territory, the ark reached Beth-shemesh. After seventy people there had violated the inmost sanctuary of the ark and paid with their lives for their curiosity, the symbol of Israel found a resting-place at Kirjath-jearim before it was finally brought to the City of David.

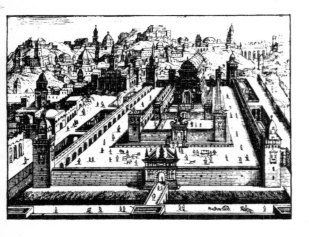

How amiable are thy tabernacles, O Lord of hosts! My soul longeth, yea, even fainteth for the courts of the Lord: my heart and my flesh crieth out for the living God. (PSALM 84, 2, 3)

The Temple of Solomon; a Renaissance reconstruction.

The kingdom which Saul had founded, David had unified and Solomon had raised to international status, disintegrated after his death (c. 922). Though the loss of the north-east part of the kingdom with Damascus was heavy (it had been brought about by the rebellions of a certain Rezon), it was not its weakened political condition that caused the fall of the kingdom, but the increasing burden of taxation and the endless forced labour. Solomon had trampled beneath his feet the people's deep-rooted love of freedom.

THE TEMPLE

...See now,
I dwell in an house of cedar, but the ark of God dwelleth within curtains.

(II SAM. 7, 2)

Thus King David to Nathan the prophet. He made all the provisions for the building of a Temple in Jerusalem which would take the place of the tabernacle and sanctuary at Shiloh. But as a warrior, he had to forgo the building of the Temple. Solomon, the king of peace, was destined for that task.

It took seven years to build the inner sanctuary, artists and craftsmen from Phoenicia being brought in for the purpose. The lines of the Temple had a noble simplicity; it was a long building with a narrow ambulatory built on to three of its sides which, being lower than the main building, formed a kind of step round it. Ten steps led up to the east-facing, splendidly decorated entrance of cypress wood with the two free-standing bronze pillars, Jachin and Boaz. Beyond the entrance was the brightly lit vestibule of the Temple, the *ullam*; adjacent to it was the richly panelled main hall, the *hechal*, into which the light percolated through small windows high up near the roof and was reflected in the polished golden lamps, basins and cups. Besides these temple furnishings, the *hechal* also contained the table of the shewbread, and a small gilded altar of cedarwood. Some steps led up to the raised end room of the Temple, the Holy of Holies (*debir*), which was shrouded in complete darkness— 'the Lord said that he would dwell in thick darkness'. For the invisible divine presence, the Holy of Holies, contained only the ark with the Law of God, over which rose up the two golden cherubim whose outspread wings extended from wall to wall. Neither idol nor statue was erected there.

Only priests were allowed into the Temple. Every Sabbath they replaced the shewbreads, of which there were twelve, a pledge of the covenant with the twelve tribes of Israel; they brought oil for the lamps and aromatic incense for the altar. Once a year, on the Day of Atonement, the High Priests entered the Holy of Holies.

The people offered up their sacrifices in the large court of the Temple where they celebrated the religious feasts. Before the Temple stood the altar of burnt offering and the 'brazen sea', a huge bronze basin held up by twelve bronze bulls, the edge of which was shaped like a lily in full bloom.

The Temple was erected on a very ancient site—over the 'holy rock' of Mount Moriah, one of the holy high places going back to Canaanite times. According to a later, but not very plausible tradition, it was the site where Abraham was about to sacrifice his son Isaac. It is the site of Ornan the Jebusite's threshing-floor, bought by David for the building of the Temple. Today the rock bears the Islamic shrine of the Dome of the Rock.

THE DIVIDED KINGDOM

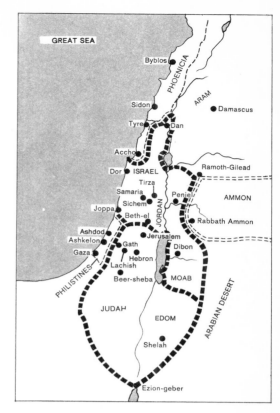

The kingdoms of Israel and Judah.

With Jeroboam, the instigator of rebellion among the northern tribes, the old rivalry between the Israelite tribes of the north and the Judaean tribes of the south flared up again. Whereas Israel could boast superiority in size and numbers, extending her ten tribes over a much larger area, and also having military superiority in the possession of chariot towns such as Megiddo and Hazor, Judah possessed the advantage of a unified population (the admixture of the Canaanite element was only slight) and a stricter form of government. But it was not only because of her good political organization that she kept faith with the house of David whose arrogant descendant Rehoboam she crowned king; the home of the royal dynasty, Judah had enjoyed a privileged position, especially under Solomon, and had been exempt from many of the burdens under which the northern tribes were groaning. Hence the Southern Kingdom confirmed Rehoboam's succession, while Israel raised the rebel Jeroboam to the throne. Thereafter, Israel and Judah each had her separate history.

Fear of Solomon had at one time driven Jeroboam to take refuge at the court of Egypt, where all Israel's enemies were made welcome. He had returned after the king's death to reap the fruits of his revolt. He developed Sichem in Ephraim and Peniel (Penuel) on the Jabbok in East Jordan as centres of government, and later on Tirzah, assumed to have been north-east of Sichem, became the royal seat in Israel. Jeroboam's most significant political act was to disassociate himself from Jerusalem's Temple cult. Since the time of the Judges there had been a sanctuary having its own cult at Dan on the northern border. He set about building another sanctuary at Beth-el on the southern border of Israel, and in both he set up images of bulls derisively described as 'the golden calves of Jeroboam'. He also appointed priests who where not members of the tribe of Levi and so broke with the religious tradition which, since the time of Aaron, had restricted the service of the cult to Levites; he also made changes in the dates of holy feast days. The last tie with Jerusalem, the true religious centre for all the tribes, had been broken. It was soon after this that war broke out between Israel and Judah.

If the northern tribes had hoped to experience the dawn of a new freedom under Jeroboam's rule, they were bitterly disappointed. Building operations and warfare did nothing to ease the burden of taxation or forced labour, the only thing that might have justified the existence of a Northern Kingdom. The internal disruption of Israel can be gauged from the rapid and bloody turnover of its ruling houses: Nadab, the son of Jeroboam, was murdered by Baasha, and the latter's son Ela by Shimri who, after seven days' reign, set fire to the royal palace at Tirzah and threw himself into the flames so as not to fall into the hands of Omri, general of the murdered king Ela. The nineteen kings who reigned in Israel over two hundred years belonged to nine different dynasties, only two of which show a certain continuity of succession—those of Omri and Jehu. By contrast, Judah's twenty kings over 335 years were all, with one exception, descendants of David.

...my father also chastised you with whips, but I will chastise you with scorpions.

(I KINGS 12, 14)

Such was Rehoboam's answer to the plea of the twelve tribes that their yoke should be lightened.

Rehoboam (922–915 B.C.), King Solomon's son, was the last king of the united kingdom and was the first ruler of the Southern Kingdom of Judah after the northern tribes under Jeroboam had refused to crown him King of Israel in Sicham.

Detail from the fresco 'Rehoboam receiving the Israelite Envoys' by Hans Holbein the Younger (1530).

After the victory of the Assyrian king Shalmaneser III over Hazael of Aram (841), Israel's King Jehu, immediately threatened by Shalmaneser, came to terms with him and paid tribute. The Bible does not mention Jehu's payment of tribute. But Shalmaneser's 'black obelisk'—a sort of victory column having on each of its four sides a series of five reliefs depicting the payment of tribute by the envoys of different regions—shows Jehu or his representative humbly kissing the ground before the Assyrian overlord's feet (see below). In the inscription on the obelisk, Jehu (who murdered the last Omrid) is described as 'the son of Omri'. Even the Assyrian Sargon II, who conquered Samaria in 721 B.C., still refers to Israel as the 'House of Omri', evidence of the extent to which Omri's rule and that of his dynasty had left its mark in Assyria.

Relief; second register of the black basalt obelisk (ninth century B.C.).

The disintegration of the kingdom occurred in an epoch when other major powers were gaining in strength. The respite which had been conducive to the establishment of the Davidian kingdom was over and the struggle for supremacy in the Near East with its valuable caravan routes was resumed. The first to attack was the Pharaoh Sheshonk I, the Shishak of the Bible. He invaded Judah in about 918 B.C., conquered and sacked one town after another, and Jerusalem was only able to save herself by handing over valuable furnishings from the Temple. Jeroboam, who had welcomed Shishak's attack on Judah, did not fare better himself; quite disregarding Jeroboam's status as his relation (he had married a cousin of the Pharaoh), Shishak pressed on into the centre of Israel and laid waste the land. After Shishak's attempt to restore Egyptian hegemony in the Near East, the threat from the south remained in abeyance for the next three hundred years. The wave of conquest which sealed the fate of Israel came from the north.

Israel which, since the time of Jeroboam, had been endeavouring to obtain control over both kingdoms, could only combat Judah so long as she was left in peace by her northern neighbour, the Aramean kingdom of Damascus. Aram in her turn could conduct her wars against Israel only if Assyria, the rising power in northern Mesopotamia, was not threatening to attack, so that Aram had sufficient respite to cover her rear while seeking to enlarge her territory in the south. And even Assyria had to cease her forays in the south when attacked by her northern neighbour Urartu (later Armenia). It was a chain of interdependence that made of yesterday's enemies the allies of today: Israel, which had been exposed to the attacks of the Arameans for over 150 years, joined forces with them against their common enemy Assyria; Judah, after nearly fifty years of enmity with Israel, helped her opponent in the war against Moab. But the short-lived alliances were only interruptions of deep-seated rivalries. Israel would no doubt have succumbed to the severe pressure from Aram had the Omrids not succeeded in giving a different turn to events.

Omri (876–869), the founder of the dynasty, whose name continued to resound in Assyrian annals long after his dynasty had come to a violent end, took over the government of a land decimated by a continuous fratricidal war. He sought peace. He granted trading rights to Aram in his newly-founded capital of Samaria. The city was built on territory not before settled, and thenceforward was to be the seat of the Israelite kings. He put an end to the senseless war between Israel and Judah in which neither state had been able to achieve supremacy. In the same way as King Solomon had reached a trade agreement with the Phoenician king Hiram I of Tyre, Omri concluded a treaty with the Phoenician regent Ithobal (Ethbaal), all the closer for the marriage between their children Jezebel and Ahab. Under Omri's skilful leadership the country experienced an economic and cultural revival, but one from which only the upper castes benefited. He even achieved military successes in the reconquest of Moab which had broken away after the division of the kingdom.

Unlike his father Omri, Ahab (869–850) took over the government of a flourishing country. He enlarged and fortified Samaria, built a luxurious palace, the 'house of ivory' of the Bible, and increased the number of his chariots. When the Arameans again attacked under their king Ben-hadad II, they were decisively beaten at the Battle of Aphek in the plain of Jezreel, and Ahab in his turn obtained trading privileges in Damascus. He showed an understanding of the needs of the hour in seeking a reconciliation after his victory with Ben-hadad and marching with him against Assyria. But his chivalry was ill-requited. Ben-hadad broke his promise to return the towns conquered by his father in East Jordan. Although warned against doing so by the prophet Michah, Ahab with his ally Josaphat, king of Judah, marched against Ramoth-Gilead which was occupied by the Arameans. He failed to recapture it and the attempt cost Ahab his life. Bleeding from severe wounds, he remained, until he died, standing in his chariot so that the people should not lose heart. Ahab's son Joram, the last Omrid, fell a victim to the bloody rebellion of his general Jehu. After a short reign filled with wars against Moab and Aram fate overtook him, though his was not the fault. It was the fault of Jezebel and Ahab.

Like many women of foreign birth, Jezebel brought the cult of her god, Melkart-Baal, to her new home. But not content with quietly worshipping her god, she looked for converts and did what she could to suppress the worship of Jahveh by persecuting his prophets. This brought about a reaction of the faithful, and the prophet Elijah challenged the 'prophets of Baal four hundred and fifty, and the prophets of the groves four hundred, which eat at Jezebel's table' to submit to God's judgement on Mount Carmel. Jahveh triumphed and the priests of Baal were killed.

The end of the Omrids was, according to the Bible, the result of their misdeeds. Fulfilling God's command, the prophet Elisha, Elijah's successor, had Jehu the general anointed king in 842 B.C. and he, following the custom of the time, wiped out all members of the previous dynasty: Joram and his family, and even the house of the king of Judah, Ahaziah who, through his mother Athaliah, was related to Ahab. Evidently Jehu also succeeded in suppressing the Baal cult in the country; from contemporary clay fragments with lists of names we see that those having Baal as a component become less frequent. Meanwhile the victory of Shalmaneser III over King Hazael of Aram (841) brought the danger of an attack on Israel uncomfortably close. Jehu bought peace by the payment of a high tribute.

But under Jeroboam II (786–746), the fourth king of the house of Jehu, Israel experienced a final and unexpected recovery. With the exclusion of Judah, Jeroboam II commanded an area which was almost equal to that of Solomon's kingdom. When the long reign of this successful monarch came to an end, destiny took its inexorable course.

Jezebel's fateful influence on the king made itself increasingly felt. When Ahab was unable to buy Naboth's vineyard, which the latter regarded as the sacred inheritance of his fathers, Jezebel was given a free hand, accused Naboth of blaspheming the king and had him stoned to death, thus permitting the king to take over the vineyard he desired.

And Elijah came unto
all the people, and said,
How long halt ye
between two opinions?
If the Lord be God,
follow him:
but if Baal,
then follow him.
And the people
answered him not a word.

(I KINGS 18, 21)

ASSYRIA AS A WORLD POWER

At the time of the divided kingdom the name Ashur—Assyria—was enough to arouse mortal terror in the world of the Near East. There are numerous accounts describing the cruel warfare of her kings. According to the annals of Shalmaneser III (858–824 B.C.) he was the first Assyrian king with whom Israel and Judah had come in contact. To stop the advance of their common enemy, ten kings of Syrian city-states and King Ahab of Israel had formed themselves into a coalition under the supreme command of the Aramean Ben-hadad II of Damascus. Their encounter with Shalmaneser at the Battle of Karkar on the Orontes (853) was not altogether unsuccessful, for Shalmaneser's 'victory' had no immediate consequences as far as the allies were concerned.

The Bible says nothing of this battle, although it temporarily banished the threat from Assyria. But it relates in detail the campaigns of Tiglath-pileser III (745–727) who ascended the throne at a time when Israel, torn by an internecine struggle for power after the death of her last strong king, Jeroboam II, had been reduced to impotence. One usurper after another seized the throne after murdering his pre-

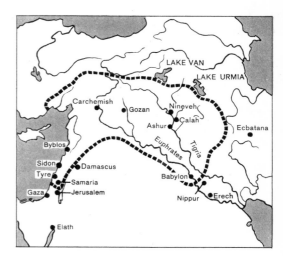

The Assyrian kingdom under the dominion of Shalmaneser III.

And Pul (Tiglath-pileser III),
the king of Assyria came against the
land:
and Menahem gave Pul a thousand
talents of silver, that his hand
might be with him to confirm
the kingdom in his hand.

(II KINGS 15, 19)

In the days of Pekah king of Israel came Tiglath-pileser king of Assyria and took Ijon, and Abel-beth-maachah, and Janoah, and Kedesh and Hazor... and carried them captive to Assyria.

(II KINGS 15, 29)

The reign of Tiglath-pileser III (745–727 B.C.), in which the New Assyrian empire rose to become a major power, was a period of wars, sometimes with the object of consolidating his own kingdom, and sometimes directed towards the conquest of independent kingdoms in Syria and Palestine. This marked the beginning of the end of the state of Israel.

Detail from a relief of the Assyrian ruler from Nimrud (eighth century B.C.).

And the Ammonites gave gifts (taxes) to Uzziah. (II CHRONICLES 26, 8)

According to an Assyrian inscription, Tiglath-pileser III fought against a Syrian coalition under the leadership of one 'Azarjau of Jaudu' (Azariah of Judah?). This account would confirm the Bible reference to Ammon.

CAPTIONS TO COLOUR PLATES

Page 57: Gift offerings from the time of the Israelite kings: clay figurines of Astarte.

Pages 58/59: Solomon's pillars in the Negev. In the time of that monarch, copper was found in the Arabah as it is today.

Page 60: Dawn on the coast of Eilat—in the distance, Aqaba in Transjordan.

decessor, the two kings Menahem and Hosea retaining it only by the favour of Assyria and in return for extortionate tribute. When Hosea, counting on Egypt's help in case of war, withheld tribute from Tiglath-pileser's successor, Shalmaneser V, he was thrown into prison. The beleaguered capital, Samaria, held out for three years, and its resistance was broken only by Shalmaneser's successor, Sargon II (721–705). With the fall of Samaria in 721 B.C. the Northern Kingdom came to an end.

The oft-told tale of the abduction of the ten tribes may have originated partly from a misreading of Assyrian policy in partially resettling conquered peoples. There is no doubt that those deported by Tiglath-pileser III were followed by the 27,290 inhabitants of Samaria, who, according to the annals of Sargon II, were settled somewhere—Gozan in northern Mesopotamia has been suggested—on the borders of the Assyrian empire where they became assimilated with the native population. If there were in fact ten tribes in Israel at the time of its disintegration—Israel is addressed by the prophet Hosea as 'Ephraim'—then Assyria would have forfeited the tribute by deporting them, for it could only be paid by a populous country. Settlers of foreign origin were taken to Israel to replace the banished tribes and the country became an Assyrian province under a governor. These were measures which precluded any future resurgence of the people.

JUDAH ALONE

That Judah did not share the fate of the Northern Kingdom was due not only to the fact that the buffer states, Aram and Israel, took the brunt of the Assyrian attack, but also to her own attitude towards Assyria, a policy going back probably to the last years of King Azariah (c. 783–742 B.C.), the most gifted and prudent monarch Judah had ever known. Azariah was successful in reincorporating into his kingdom Edom with its port Ezion-geber (Eilat), which had earlier been lost to Judah, and in this way he gained control of the most important trade routes from the Mediterranean to Egypt and Arabia; he even made Ammon tributary. Uzziah was excluded from active rule by a terrible disease, leprosy, and from his total segregation all he could do was to give guidance and advice to his son and co-regent Jotham, and later to his grandson Ahaz.

Both Jotham and Ahaz refrained from taking part in alliances against Assyria. No doubt their policy preserved Judah from Assyrian retaliation, but it also exposed the Southern Kingdom to the revenge of those who had allied themselves against Assyria. When Ahaz refused to join a coalition against that country, Pekah of Israel and Rezon of Damascus joined forces and marched to the gates of Jerusalem. The promise of valuable gifts induced King Tiglath-pileser of Assyria to come to the assistance of the threatened city, and Damascus was overthrown in 732 B.C. In spite of the destruction Judah had suffered from the inroads of Philistines and Edomites instigated by Pekah and Rezon, in the event her submission to Assyrian power proved salutary. But this, too, brought another risk; Judah was flooded with Assyrian cults which even led to the desecration of the Temple. Ahaz succumbed to this hazard—Hezekiah, his successor, overcame it.

Hezekiah (715–686), the man of faith, is accorded by the Bible the greatest honour that can be conferred on any king—he is compared with David. After the fall of Samaria, which took place during his reign, he tried to attract the population of Israel back to the Temple by acknowledging the changes they had made in the dates of feast-days. But it was Hezekiah, too, who reversed the policy of his predecessors towards Assyria, entering into a secret alliance with the Philistine cities of Ekron and Ashkelon which, like the Phoenician towns of Tyre and Sidon, were centres of revolt against Assyrian supremacy.

The rebellion was sparked off by the Chaldean Merodach-Baladan, who had seized the throne of Babylon (721) and by so doing had given the signal for other peoples to throw off the Assyrian yoke. In spite of the military aid which the rising received from the Pharaoh Shabaka, Sennacherib (705–681), son of Sargon II and successor to the Assyrian throne, was able to subdue the rebellious towns of Phoenicia and Philistia. Hezekiah had no more allies to whom he could turn for help when in 701 B.C. Sennacherib took the fortress of Lachish in south Judah and advanced to besiege Jerusalem. It was a desperate situation from which the city was saved by a miracle; Sennacherib raised the siege. It is debatable whether an epidemic had broken out in the army, as is maintained by the Greek historian Herodotus, or whether Hezekiah was forced to submit and to buy himself out with a heavy tribute. Whatever the case, however, Judah had to pay heavily for her attempted rebellion. Part of the land was handed over to Philistine cities which had remained loyal to the Assyrians, and many of her inhabitants were deported.

Manasseh, Hezekiah's successor, showed himself once more an obedient vassal of Assyria and the Temple was thrown open to Assyrian cults which, during the long reign of Manasseh, completely overlaid the cult of Jahveh. In Josiah (640–609) the country then found one of its greatest reformers. The motive behind the fundamental reform of the Jahveh religion and the centralization of the whole cult in Jerusalem was a 'Book of the Law' of venerable age that had been discovered during repairs to the Temple building (622). Its reading made a tremendous impact on the people who, as a result, found their way back to their God. The subsequent Feast of the Passover, when all the faithful assembled in Jerusalem, was in effect a renewal of Jahveh's covenant with his people.

Meanwhile the great powers were engaged in a struggle of unprecedented scope and violence. Assyria had been strong enough to eliminate her most powerful rival, Egypt, but under the blows of the northern people, the Medes and Scythians, the giant showed signs of weakening and when in 612 B.C. Nineveh, the Assyrian capital, was destroyed by the Chaldean Nabopolassar, the struggle for power had been settled in favour of the Neo-Babylonian Kingdom, whose first king he became. What happened next was unforeseen: the Pharaoh Necho (609–593) came to the assistance of his rival, Assyria, now no longer dangerous and a welcome ally against Babylon. Josiah, like his predecessor Hezekiah, was on the side of Babylon; he marched out to meet Necho in order to prevent him joining up with Assyria. There was a battle at Megiddo (609) in which Josiah lost his life. For four years Judah was Necho's vassal state; King Johoahaz, a son of Josiah, was banished to Egypt and was replaced by his more acceptable brother Jehoiachim (Eliakim).

But Egyptian supremacy came to an abrupt end when Nabopolassar's son, the crown prince Nebuchadnezzar, at the Battle of Carchemish in 605 B.C. won a decisive victory over Necho and gained control over the territory occupied by the latter. Jehoiachim, now a vassal of Babylon, clung narrowly and obstinately to his pro-Egyptian policy, rebelled against Nebuchadnezzar (604–562) and ruthlessly persecuted anyone who, like the prophet Jeremiah, counselled moderation.

And he (Hezekiah) did that
which was right
in the sight of the Lord,
according to all
that David his father did.

(II KINGS 18, 3)

Now in the fourteenth year of king Hezekiah did Sennacherib king of Assyria come up against all the fenced cities of Judah, and took them. (II KINGS 18, 13)

King Sennacherib (705–681 B.C.) at Lachish, which was conquered in 701. It was Sennacherib's headquarters before he went on to beleaguer Jerusalem.

Detail from a relief in Nineveh (c. 690 B.C.).

Judah in King Hezekiah's time (c. 700 B.C.).

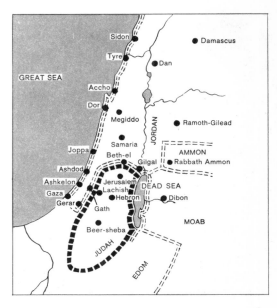

Nebuchadnezzar II (604–562 B.C.), the most important ruler to occupy the Neo-Babylonian throne, followed up his victory at Carchemish (605) over the Pharaoh Necho, with several campaigns in which he overthrew Syria and Palestine. Judah rebelled twice. Nebuchadnezzar then put an end to the state.

Nebuchadnezzar seal (c. 605 B.C.).

Nebuchadnezzar, who had repeatedly sent troops against Judah, laid siege to Jerusalem for the first time in 598 B.C. Jehoiachim died at this juncture and his successor, the young Jehoiachin, had no alternative but to open the gates of the city. He and his family, and some of the leading citizens of Judah were taken captive to Babylon.

But this was not the end. Under the new king Zedekiah (Mattaniah), another son of Josiah, the hope of liberation was revived by rumours of help from Egypt. The rebellion against Babylon, which flared up simultaneously in Phoenicia and East Jordan also infected Judah where the weak-minded Zedekiah became a helpless tool in the hands of opportunist rebels.

With the determination of destroying the insurgents once and for all, Nebuchadnezzar advanced against Judah in 589. Lachish was the last fortress which he conquered before he began the siege of Jerusalem. In spite of hunger and thirst the city held out against overwhelming odds for eighteen months. In 587 B.C., on 9th Ab, a fateful day for the people, the walls fell. The city was sacked and destroyed and the Temple burnt down. Judah was laid waste and her ruling caste deported to Babylon. Only a small peasant population was left. Jeremiah the prophet stayed with them.

Then said they, Come and let us devise devices against Jeremiah.... Give heed to me, O Lord, and hearken to the voice of them that contend with me. Shall evil be recompensed for good? For they have digged a pit for my soul. Remem-

ber that I stood before thee to speak good for them, and to turn away thy wrath from them... Yet, Lord, thou knowest all their counsel against me to slay me: forgive not their iniquity, neither blot out their sin from thy sight, but let them be overthrown before thee; deal thus with them in the time of thine anger.
(JEREMIAH 18, 18–20, 23)

Fresco from the ceiling of the Sistine Chapel in Rome, by Michelangelo (1475–1564).

THE TIME OF THE PROPHETS

When in the eighth century B.C. polytheistic cults threatened increasingly to strangle the worship of Jahveh and at the same time the living Jahveh religion seemed to be relapsing into rigid cultic formalism, there arose a number of spiritual leaders of immense significance to the people. These were the scriptural prophets, having nothing but the name in common with those earlier 'prophets' who first appeared towards the end of the time of the Judges, living in groups and experiencing 'visions' of the occult in ecstatic, trance-like states. Amos, Hosea, Isaiah and Jeremiah were solitaries.

They had been preceded in the ninth century by Elijah and Elisha, both of whom retained, however, characteristics of group activity, albeit in the different form of the prophetic school. Both were men of action.

The scriptural prophets, on the other hand, were men of words, with which they castigated the people, accusing them of having abandoned their God. The prophets turned against the cult of alien gods and denounced the hollow practice of religion.

To what purpose is the multitude of your sacrifices unto me? saith the Lord.... And when ye spread forth your hands, I will hide mine eyes from you: yea, when ye make many prayers, I will not hear: your hands are full of blood. Wash you, make you clean; put away the evil of your doings from before mine eyes; cease to do evil: Learn to do well; seek judgement, relieve the oppressed, judge the fatherless, plead for the widow. (ISAIAH 1, 11, 15–17)

Amos, too, used similar words. And Jeremiah warned that even the sanctuary of the people, the Temple itself, would not be God's dwelling-place so long as they persisted in sin. 'Shall I come before him with calves a year old?' asks Michah. God demands more of Israel; transgressions cannot be bought off. 'You only have I known of all the families of the earth: therefore I will punish you for all your iniquities', says Amos. This implies the election of Israel.

The prophets came from all ranks of the people; Amos was a shepherd, Jeremiah the son of a priest. They had been 'called' by God, that is the basic meaning of the word *Nebiim*, prophets. Like Moses, they attempted to evade their mission, which is felt as a 'burden' *(ol)*. Their calling needed courage and commitment. Unwaveringly they recalled to the people the pledge of Sinai, and called the king to task for every misdeed, without fear or equivocation. God's judgement on the faithless people is depicted with poetic vigour and in tones of anguish they are called upon to repent and reform.

Amos proclaims God's wrath, Hosea his merciful love. Isaiah announces the advent of the Messianic era when the purified world will be blessed.

> Come, and let us return
> unto the Lord:
> for he hath torn,
> and he will heal us;
> he hath smitten
> and he will bind us up.
>
> (HOSEA 6, 1)

IN BABYLON

> By the rivers of Babylon, there we sat down,
> yea, we wept, when we remembered Zion.
> If I forget thee, O Jerusalem, let my right hand
> forget her cunning.
>
> (PSALM 137, 1, 5)

These words echo the suffering and nostalgia of those who had been carried off to Babylon.

There are few sources from the early part of their exile. Such as there are show that the Judeans, although they had freedom of movement, probably had to do forced labour. After a considerable lapse of time, however—no doubt after the death of Nebuchadnezzar in 562 B.C.—their conditions were greatly mitigated; they probably formed their own communities, and the very prosperous country, then at the height of its material and spiritual development, offered them every opportunity, according to Babylonian records, of attaining a position of standing and of earning a fortune.

Yet they did not become assimilated with their surroundings, nor did they succumb to the attraction of Babylonian cults. They regarded their deportation from their homeland as a well-merited punishment, understanding now the warnings of the prophets and listening to their words. It was Ezekiel who condemned all straying from the faith, and whose imaginative language gave expression to the certainty of the people's rebirth. It was largely due to him and to that anonymous prophet, the 'second Isaiah', known to us only from his writings (ISAIAH 40–55), that the people found their way back to their faith. Their assemblies, in which they had been used to

And Haman said unto King Ahasuerus, There is a certain people scattered abroad and dispersed... and their laws are diverse from all people.... If it please the king, let it be written that they may be destroyed: and I will pay ten thousand talents of silver... to bring it into the king's treasuries.... And the king said unto Haman, The silver is given to thee, the people also, to do with them as it seemeth good to thee. (ESTHER 3, 8, 9, 11)

Warned by her uncle, Mordecai, of the danger that was threatening, Queen Esther, the clever wife of Ahasuerus, was able to foil Haman's plan to kill in one day every Jew in the kingdom of Persia. To celebrate their lucky escape, the Jewish people annually hold a cheerful masquerade, Purim ('Lot').

Ahasuerus has been identified as the Persian king Xerxes I (486–465 B.C.). The account is legendary, but very typical of the fate of the Jews.

Esther goes to the king. Painting by Filippino Lippi (1457–1504).

Cyrus II (559–530 B.C.), one of the greatest conquerors in the ancient world and founder of the Persian empire. Wood engraving (eighteenth century).

Thus saith Cyrus king of Persia,
The Lord God of heaven hath given
me all the kingdoms of the earth;
and he hath charged me to build him
an house at Jerusalem, which is in
Judah. Who is there among you
of all his people? His God be with him,
and let him go up to Jerusalem,
which is in Judah, and build the house
of the Lord God of Israel,
(he is the God) which is in Jerusalem.
And whosoever remaineth in any
place where he sojourneth, let the men
of his place help him with silver,
and with gold, and with goods,
and with beasts, beside the freewill
offering for the house of God that is in
Jerusalem... and let the expenses
be given out of the king's house:
And also let the golden and silver
vessels of the house of God, which
Nebuchadnezzar took forth out of
the temple which is at Jerusalem, and
brought unto Babylon, be restored,
and brought again unto the temple
which is at Jerusalem, every one to
his place, and place them in the house
of God.   (EZRA 1, 2–4; 6, 4, 5)

Modern historical research has shown that in style and form this decree corresponds to the documents of the Persian king; the fact that it is written in Aramaic, the diplomatic language of the western part of the Persian empire, also suggests that this is Cyrus' decree.

discuss community matters and to exchange memories, now served for prayer and teaching. Thus arose the synagogue, the Jews' modest house of prayer. Without a country, bound to their God, they remained a people even in exile. Although oppression had long ceased, many of them looked to a return to their former home. A prophet, that same second Isaiah, promises the return and names their liberator:

> ...That saith of Cyrus (Cyrus II), He is my shepherd, and shall perform all my pleasure: even saying to Jerusalem, Thou shalt be built; and to the temple, Thy foundation shall be laid. (ISAIAH 44, 28)

THE RETURN HOME

Cyrus II (559–530) of the Persian dynasty of Achaemenidae, dethroned Astyages, the last king of the Medes, thus uniting Media and Persia; a little later he overran Lydia (546) and then turned against Babylon which, in 539 B.C., after the total defeat of a Babylonian army, submitted without resistance. The rise of the Persian empire had brought to an end the Neo-Babylonian Kingdom.

As a conqueror, Cyrus showed rare political acumen. He pacified subject peoples by granting them a considerable degree of autonomy and even protected and encouraged their cultural traditions. Peoples who had been deported by Assyrian and Babylonian rulers were given leave to return home. By a decree of 538 B.C., the Jews were allowed to rebuild their Temple in Jerusalem.

According to the Bible, fifty thousand immediately followed the call to return home. But it is likely that this number is based on a later census and comprises all the Jews who, in the course of several generations, followed in the wake of the first home-comers.

The supervision of the building of the Temple was entrusted by Cyrus to one Sheshbazzar. All that is known of this man is that he had taken charge of the Temple furnishing looted by Nebuchadnezzar and was again in charge of them when Cyrus returned them to Jerusalem. Those who had come back began by setting up the altar for burnt offerings on the Temple site and about a year later the rebuilding commenced. They rejected the proffered help of the Samaritans, descendants of Israelites who had remained in the country after the fall of Samaria and had become assimilated with other races, for they feared the influence of their adulterated religion. The subsequent attitude of the Samaritans, so hostile that it did not stop short at denunciation to the Persian king, delayed the work. In addition the people were crushed by the exceptionally arduous struggle for existence, and their strength was sapped by toil and privation. The work, barely begun, came to a halt.

It was the burning oratory of the prophets Haggai and Zechariah that caused the work to be resumed. Darius I (521–486) endorsed Cyrus' original decree, at the same time making provision for the cost of building and the upkeep of the cult. And when under Zerubbabel, the Persian representative from the house of David, the now completed Temple was dedicated in 515 B.C., it had become the cult centre not only for those who lived in the country, but for all Jews dispersed throughout the world.

But the people had not really reestablished themselves in the country before the time of the priest and scribe Ezra, who probably arrived in Jerusalem in 458 B.C., and Nehemiah, the cup-bearer of the Persian king Artaxerxes I (465–424), appointed by his master in 445 governor of Judah, a province independent of Samaria. While Nehemiah was concerned essentially with the administrative organization of the province and sought to abolish political and social abuses, Ezra's reforms applied chiefly to religious life, reconstituting the cultic communities of Jerusalem on the basis of the Law.

Particular problems were presented by mixed marriages and the practice of usury by the rich. Both men, Ezra and Nehemiah, forbade the people in future to enter into marriage with women of neighbouring races. It was rare for an extant mixed marriage to be forcibly dissolved. But their undertaking bore less fruit than they had hoped. On the other hand Nehemiah's persuasive powers led wealthy citizens to remit all debts. Previously they had all too often forced the destitute to sell their children into slavery. Nehemiah himself gave up all his possessions and did not take his salary as governor.

In spite of the neighbours' hostility, walls were built round the Holy City in the time of Nehemiah, and all participated in erecting them. The government lay in the hands of a 'Council of Elders' headed by the High Priest. For a century the people lived peacefully under Persian rule. Then a new conqueror appeared.

But it came to pass, that when Sanballat, and Tobiah, and the Arabians, and the Ammonites, and the Ashdodites, heard that the walls of Jerusalem were made up, and that the breaches began to be stopped, then they were very wroth... and the rulers were behind all the house of Judah. They which builded on the wall... every one with one of his hands wrought in the work, and with the other hand held a weapon.

(NEHEMIAH 4, 7, 16, 17)

Since the return from Babylon, nearly two and a half millennia have passed....

Alexander the Great (356–323 B.C.), son of Philip II of Macedon, who was educated by his great tutor Aristotle, conquered the east not only as general but also as propagator of Hellenism. According to a Talmudic legend, Alexander behaved with deference towards the High Priest who went out from Jerusalem to meet the conqueror. When he was asked why, Alexander replied that the venerable man had appeared to him in a dream, and had led him to victory.

Tetradrachm with Alexander the Great's portrait, struck at Acre.

THE HELLENISTIC PERIOD

The world was holding its breath: Alexander, the youth who occupied the Macedonian throne, had put to flight the great Persian king, Darius III in a dashing cavalry attack at Issus. That was in 333 B.C. Two years later the Persian empire had been overpowered by the foreign conqueror. From that time on, the actions of this restless king were all dictated by one idea—to combine the manner of life of the Macedonian-Greek peoples with that of the Irano-Persians. The founding of numerous towns, among them Alexandria in Egypt, later to be internationally important, soon propagated Greek culture and the Greek language. A new epoch in world history was beginning.

After Alexander's early death (323), none of the possible successors was able to complete the construction of the world empire as their king had planned it. The empire distintegrated and was replaced, after many ups and downs and ferocious battles, by the world of Hellenistic states. Alexander's generals shared out the dominions amongst themselves.

Like Alexander, the Ptolemies, so called after Ptolemy I, respected the Jews' traditional way of life for the next hundred years of their rule in Egypt and Palestine. During that time many Jewish emigrants sought a second home in Egypt, especially in the Ptolemaic royal city of Alexandria which, along with Jerusalem, was to become a centre of Jewish life. It was there that the holy scriptures were translated into Greek, the Egyptian Jews having adopted Greek as their everyday language. The Greek Bible, the Septuagint, was fundamental not only to the Jewish intellectual world, but also to Christianity and its propagation.

After Alexander's death in 323 B.C. his kingdom disintegrated and after bloody struggles his succession was divided up among his generals. Egypt fell to the Ptolemies, whose dynasty begins with Ptolemy I Soter (died 283), and the Asiatic section of Alexander's empire to the Seleucids, named after the dynasty's founder, Seleucus I Nicator. But after the Battle of Ipsus (301), Ptolemy succeeded in gaining dominion over Palestine and Phoenicia; as a result the country was ruled during the third century by his benevolent successors. Ptolemy, too, was a historian, and our best available source for the campaigns of Alexander.

Bust of Ptolemy I (323–283 B.C.).

In memory of the year 164 B.C. when the Temple was dedicated, the Jewish people annually celebrate the eight days' feast of Hanucah (Dedication). Legend has it that the small amount of consecrated oil found in the Temple, which should have been enough for only one day, went on burning for a week.

In Judea the Greeks' more civilized way of life, their science and philosophy, exercised an irresistible attraction on the leading castes and soon an ominous gap yawned between them and those remaining faithful to the Law, the *Hasidim*. Judea might also have gradually become partially hellenized had not the violent measures of the cruel and unpredictable Seleucid king Antiochus IV Epiphanes (175–163) caused the people to resist. His father Antiochus III, who had put an end to Ptolemaic rule in Palestine in 198 and who had set up the Seleucids, had not intervened in Judea's internal affairs, and had even granted privileges to Jerusalem. But his son forbade circumcision and the keeping of the Sabbath under pain of death, caused the Books of Law to be burned, made the worship of Greek gods compulsory throughout the land and finally set up a sacrificial altar to Zeus in the Temple itself (168).

This final excess outraged the people's innermost feelings. When the venerable priest, Mattathias of Modein, refused to make the sacrifice, even killing a Jew who was preparing to do so, rebellion flared up under the leadership of the third of his five sons, Judas Maccabaeus. The Hasidim, whose earlier passive resistance had only served to arouse the murderous instincts of the king, flocked to join the rebellion, and soon the whole country was in a state of revolt. Armies were sent from Syria, the heart of the Seleucid kingdom, to fight the rebels. At the beginning the Jews would not fight on the Sabbath, nor would they defend themselves, until their losses became so severe that they were forced to suspend the consecration of the seventh day. Deriving strength from their religious zeal, Judas and his warriors overcame the vastly superior forces of the enemy and took Jerusalem in 164. The rededication of the Temple took place on the third anniversary of its desecration.

Now that the fight for religious freedom had been won, the fight for independence began. This struggle, too, was brought to a successful conclusion when Simon, the last remaining son of Mattathias, was able to drive the Syrian troops out of Jerusalem's citadel and conclude an agreement with the Seleucid Demetrius II, which exempted Judea from tribute. In gratitude, the people invested Simon with the hereditary office of High Priest, so giving rise to the Hasmonean dynasty in 140 B.C. Its founding revived old dreams of restoring the splendour of the Davidian kingdom. Simon's son, John Hyrcanus I, was a distinctly warlike prince, who surrounded himself with the pomp of a Hellenistic-oriental ruler; his grandson, Aristobulus I assumed the title of king, and his successor, Alexander Jannaeus (103–76), a power-politician like every other king in the Near East, did in fact restore the kingdom's frontiers almost as they had been under David.

But the internecine feuds which had long been smouldering between *Sadducees* and *Pharisees* finally exploded. The Sadducees belonged to the priestly aristocracy, the caste of rich merchants and landowners; the Pharisees, probably deriving from the Hasidim, belonged to the people's party that adhered to the Law; by their interpretation of the Law, their scribes had set up a framework within which all questions in the daily life of the individual were regulated. The Pharisees hotly supported the need for leadership of the people by a worthy High Priest and his council, and were strongly opposed to the power politics of Alexander Jannaeus whose death they demanded. The civil war they precipitated lasted six years (93–87) and caused the death of fifty thousand people. Only after the death of Alexander Jannaeus, did the country once again experience peace under the most capable rule of his widow, Salome Alexandra (76–67).

After her death, her sons Hyrcanus II, who held the office of High Priest, and Aristobulus II, contested the succession. The Idumean (Edomite) Antipater, inflamed the quarrel and a war broke out which neither of the brothers won; the victor was the Roman, Pompey. Both had called on him for help, and in 65 B.C., after embittered fighting, he was master of the situation. He made of Judea a Roman protectorate. For the Hasmoneans the play was over. Hyrcanus, indeed, remained High Priest of the country, but he was a tributary vassal prince; Aristobulus was taken to Rome and compelled to appear in Pompey's triumph. Antigonus, the last member of the dynasty, was murdered in 37 B.C. The order was given by the son of Antipater, Herod, the first king of the Jews under Roman rule.

UNDER ROMAN RULE

With the fall of Jerusalem and its Temple to Pompey (65 B.C.) and the establishment of Roman hegemony over the country and throughout the Near East, a period of intense political and religious ferment began, punctuated by frequent and sudden revolts; it was to shake the very foundations of national existence. Since the time of the Babylonian captivity it had not undergone so severe a test. The culmination came with the Jewish War (A.D. 66–70), the destruction of Jerusalem and the final loss of national sovereignty.

We are better informed about the dramatic events of this time than about any other epoch of Jewish history. This we owe to Flavius Josephus, the Jewish historian, who was not only an eye-witness of the war, but himself played a decisive role in events as leader and organizer of the revolt in Galilee.

Whereas almost all other peoples of the ancient world bowed more or less voluntarily to the yoke of the Roman empire, only two oriental races, the Parthians and the Jews, effectively resisted alien rule in an almost constant series of rebellions.

The demotic monarchy of the Hasmoneans was the last national sovereign dynasty in the country. The ruler held both religious and political power; he combined the roles of head of state and High Priest. After the conquest of Jerusalem by Pompey, Hyrcanus lost his royal title and his rule was confined to purely religious matters; scarcely a vestige remained of his political authority. Meanwhile Antipater and his sons Phasael and Herod became increasingly influential. And when his father fell victim to a conspiracy and his brother committed suicide, Herod seized Jerusalem in 37 with the help of Roman forces. He had the last Hasmonean, Antigonus, executed and took possession of the throne, having been nominated King of Judea by the Roman Senate.

Herod (37–4), the Idumean upstart and Roman favourite, ruled with a strong hand. He succeeded in once again uniting nearly the whole of Palestine into a single political entity. The country was at peace, and even attained a degree of prosperity from its thriving commerce. Yet Herod's internal policy was conducted through a ghastly régime of terror with an utter disregard for the people's longstanding prerogatives. The Sanhedrin (Great Council), found its judicial activity and power considerably reduced; it retained the right to make decisions only in respect of religious matters. The office of High Priest became a pawn in the political game, its incumbent being changed as often as possible whereas it was originally intended to be held for life, and the priestly robes, the insignia of office, were in the king's keeping.

Under Herod the process of Hellenization and Romanization made rapid advances: Caesarea on the Mediterranean coast was founded as a pagan town. Old Samaria was reconstructed and renamed Sebaste in honour of Augustus to whom a temple was

Herod I (37–4 B.C.), the foreign usurper favoured by Rome, described himself as 'King of the Jews', and carried on a veritable reign of terror, with a complete disregard for the Jewish people's religious and cultural tradition.

Mosaic in the baptistery of St. Marks Church, Venice (thirteenth century).

also dedicated. Even in Jerusalem a theatre and amphitheatre were built. The most magnificent building, however, was the royal palace to the west of the Upper City with its towers Phasael, Hippicus and Mariamne. Herod's two-faced loyalty which led him on the one hand, in order to please the Jews, to rebuild and enlarge the Temple with extravagant splendour, and on the other to curry favour with the Romans by erecting numerous temples in honour of pagan gods outside the country, aroused the deepest hatred of the people. It was a hatred that his unbridled cruelty further nourished. His opponents were executed or crucified in their hundreds and thousands, and he did not recoil from the murder of his own family, his wife Mariamne for instance, or his sons Alexander and Aristobulus. The loss of the national dynasty of Hasmoneans, its replacement by the reign of terror of a cruel, alien usurper supported by Rome, the disenfranchisement of the people and its representatives, the imposition of foreign customs on the national and religious tradition, all combined to rob the freedom-loving Jewish people, always given to extremes, of its national and religious consciousness. And with the loss of its healthy sense of national existence it succumbed to a condition of extreme inner turmoil and spiritual desolation. The last pre-Christian and the first post-Christian centuries, until well into the first half of the second century, witnessed almost continual disturbances. Thus immediately after Herod's death (A.D. 4) a rebellion broke out against Idumean-Roman rule in Judea, Galilee and Perea which was suppressed with unbelievable cruelty by the Roman legate, Varus.

The political unity achieved by Herod was lost by his successors, his sons Philippus, Archelaus and Antipas. They governed regions allotted to them by Augustus, the Roman emperor: Archelaus, with the title of 'Ethnarch' in Judea, Samaria and Idumea, Antipas as Tetrarch in Galilee and Perea, and Philippus as Tetrarch of the north-eastern sector of Jordan including Caesarea Philippi. The royal title, later revived in favour of Agrippa I and Agrippa II, thus disappeared.

After nine years' rule, Archelaus was deposed by Augustus for incompetence and his region came under direct Roman rule, exercised by procurators.

All three regions were inherited by Agrippa I (A.D. 37–44, king from 41), Herod's grandson. Under his mild rule, the country enjoyed one last, if brief, flowering. After his death, it reverted finally to Rome, whose procurators ruled the whole country from their centre at Caesarea. Their total lack of understanding for the *mores* and customs of the country, their shameless looting and robbery of the population and constant flouting of their religious feelings, were the fundamental causes of the impending catastrophe.

Since the time of the Hasmoneans popular opinion had been divided between the two national religious parties of the Sadducees and Pharisees. The Sadducee party was composed, as we have seen, of priests and members of wealthy castes whose main preoccupation was to uphold their own social status. In the sphere of politics and religion they therefore opposed all innovation, but as well-to-do people they were 'open-minded' and prepared to take up Graeco-Hellenistic cultural ideals. But the Pharisees, comprising the castes of the scribes, the scholars, rabbis and students, were custodians, commentators and elaborators of the Law. Both parties, however, in view of the existing political situation, were compelled to come to terms with their Roman overlords.

In spite of the Pharisees' great influence, the increasingly critical political position gave rise to extreme reactions on the part of the people. Terrorist bands of mainly young men, known as Zealots arose, first of all in Galilee. They were the real agents of revolt against Rome. But their radicalism paled beside that of the later *Sicarii* who, unrestrained by any form of morality, sought to achieve their political goals by

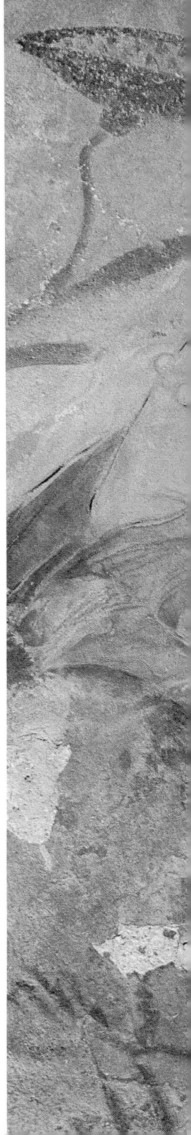

assassination. Since the time of the procurator Antonius Felix (A.D. 52–60), they had kept the country in a state of terror, and their assassinations, which usually took place where the crowd was thickest, were chiefly aimed at supporters of the Pharisees and Sadducees. These were regarded as traitors and enemies of the people, and were likewise the objects of Zealot terrorist attacks. So the people slaughtered one another in a frenzy of fratricide, which depleted their ranks to an extent that was truly terrifying even before the Roman siege in A.D. 70.

One of the consequences of the utter disruption of the country was the widespread belief that the end of the world was approaching and the Messianic kingdom imminent. This gave rise on the one hand to the appearance of false prophets and miracle workers, but on the other it brought about genuine religious manifestations which were to prove of great historical significance. Many found refuge in the solitude of the desert from the temptations of the world, and lived there a life of purity. John the Baptist is such a figure. Others withdrew into the shelter of the monkish 'Essene' communities, in order to prepare themselves for the Messianic kingdom by a life of strict religious discipline and continence. The Dead Sea finds and the Qumran excavations have shed new and surprising light on the Messianic movements of that time.

It is now considered certain that the Messianic movement of the Essenes, originating late in the second century B.C., created the necessary conditions for the rise of Christianity; there is nothing to show, however, that Christ had any direct connections with it. The gospels and the Dead Sea Scrolls have a great many points in common, in so far as they concern the sect themselves. Nevertheless there are fundamental differences: The Essenes' strict discipline which demands the subjection of younger men to their elders is not found in Christian teaching:

Palestine under Roman rule (in the time of Jesus).

> And whosoever will be chief
> among you, let him
> be your servant.
> (MATT. 20, 27)

says Jesus, and, in as much as he does not recoil from washing the feet of his disciples, the apostles, he exemplifies this.

As an ascetic congregation, the Essenes were concerned only with their own circles and would accept no hospitality outside their own society. Not so, Christ. He was open-minded and without class prejudice, although he scourged the formalism, the vanity and the hidden greed of the Pharisees in the most scathing terms. While the movement of the Essenes might appear to be an escape from the world into religion, its followers were pledged, in preparation for the kingdom of God on earth, to lead an exemplary and active life within a well-organized and strictly disciplined community in which there was no precedence except age. The community was founded on traditional religious teaching, although not taking part in Temple sacrifces and having its own calendar of the feast days. The Messianic kingdom was to be realized here on earth, not—as in the later Christian view—in another world.

THE BIRTH OF CHRISTIANITY

CHRISTIANITY AND JUDAISM

But when the fulness
of the time was come,
God sent forth his Son....

(GAL. 4, 4)

In the gospel of St. Luke (LUKE 2, 1, 2), the birth of Christ is seen in relation to the name of Augustus and the 'taxing' of Quirinius (Cyrenius). The Early Father, Eusebius (c. A.D. 260–340), saw in this a divinely pre-ordained link between empire and Christ's coming, between monarchy and monotheistic Christianity. For him, as for the Early Father Origen (c. 184–253), Augustus' rule of peace was the tool of providence and the Roman empire the very foundation of the Christian mission. And, indeed, 'when the fulness of the time was come', the *pax Augusta* (the universal peace proclaimed by Augustus in 17 B.C.), the international validity of the Greek and Latin tongues, and the uninterrupted network of communications that covered the empire from east to west, had paved the way for a universal religion. Had it not been for the agency of the Imperium Romanum and the century of imperial peace that began with Augustus (27 B.C. to A.D. 14)—the longest period of peace mankind had known up to that time—the triumphant progress of Christianity throughout the ancient world, and later through Europe, would not have been possible.

Statue of Augustus in the Vatican in Rome.

The fundamental difference between the teaching of Jesus and that of the prophets and later religious leaders is that Christ's message is universal and human, addressed to mankind as such, whereas the prophets are concerned with the Jewish people in whose social and political life they actively intervene.

Christ is not directly involved in the events of his time, in national and political affairs. He preaches straightforward obedience to the ruling power—'Render unto Ceasar the things that are Caesar's' (MATT. 22, 21). But he in no way broke with traditional Jewish Law. He himself says: 'Think not that I am come to destroy the law, or the prophets: I am not come to destroy but to fulfil. For verily I say unto you, Till heaven and earth pass, one jot or one tittle shall in no wise pass from the law, till all be fulfilled.' (MATT. 5, 17-18)

Thus throughout his life, Jesus was a Jew among Jews. His ethical demands, indeed, are to be found in the Mishnah and the Talmud in the sayings of religious teachers like Hillel and Shammai. But with Jesus they become absolute postulates which presuppose a perfect human society. In this way they are in opposition to the traditional Jewish concept of the Law which, though it takes into account the absolute ethical demand, yet in practice adapts the Law to existing national, political and human requirements. In contrast to the purely ideal ethical demands of Jesus, we have the practical legal code of the Jews which allows for existence as it is lived. The two points of view were irreconcilable.

Jesus says: 'But I say unto you, That ye resist not evil: but whosoever shall smite thee on thy right cheek, turn to him the other also. And if any man will sue thee at the law, and take away thy coat, let him have thy cloak also' (MATT. 5, 39-40). These ethical postulates demand a final self-surrender and purification of man in preparation for the imminent Messianic kingdom of God: 'Be ye therefore perfect, even as your Father which is in heaven is perfect' (MATT. 5, 48).

Man's purification is one of the basic ethical demands of Judaism from earliest times. It results from a lasting personal preoccupation with religious questions which embrace the whole of existence. Thus the learning of the Law becomes the imperative religious commandment. The Law must be fulfilled through its conscious realization and out of a deeper insight into the will of God and the existential contingency. It is the actualization in life of God.

Christ's absolute ethical postulates became the foundation of a new world religion, Christianity. It is directed to mankind in general and no longer has any national limitations. The formulation of this religion was the concern of later generations, however. Christ did not see himself as a religious founder. He was the Messiah, by whom the ages would be completed and fulfilled. Had his mission not ended in tragedy, the new religion would never have taken shape.

Its true founder was Paul, the Pharisee from Cilician Tarsus, and with him the apostles. Paul propagated the new faith throughout the world as then known. His travels took him as far as Italy, Greece, Asia Minor, and Syria, and everywhere he sought out Jewish communities—evidence for a considerable Jewish *diaspora* as early as the first century A.D.—where he proclaimed the new doctrine not to the Jews only, but to the heathen in particular.

With the spread of religion among the heathen Paul was forced to relinquish many of Judaism's restrictive laws such as those concerning circumcision, food, the Sabbath and purification. These represented the national and religious character of Judaism, but they meant little to the Graeco-Roman world. With the growth of Christianity, the figure of Jesus was held to be divine. He became the resurrected Son of God, a member of the Trinity together with God the Father and the Holy Ghost. He belonged to both the divine and the earthly world and was seen as mediator between the two.

Christ's life, passion and death henceforward became exemplary for mankind in Europe. They no longer looked to the Greek ideal of the bodily perfect, harmonious and heroic man, but to the spiritual ideal of *homo religiosus,* the humble saint who seeks redemption in another world through suffering in the earthly vale of woe.

Christ and his family, his successors the apostles, and the community of saints constitute the divine hierarchy of the church whose cult-objects they became. By their exemplary life, they have raised themselves above sinning humanity to form a kind of halfway kingdom where they act as mediators between unredeemed humanity and the eternal life of the other world. This mystical intermediary kingdom of saints finds architectonic realization on earth within the structure of the Church.

The concept of 'holiness' also derives from Judaistic teaching. Its purest and most comprehensive formulation is found in the doctrine of the One God (monotheism) already apparent in the covenant made by God with Moses. The holiness of God is more than a mere attribute such as omnipotence or absolute goodness; it is the essence of the divine being. When, in the covenant with Moses, God makes the people into a holy people and their land a holy land, it means that he allows people and land to participate in his divine being.

But such participation is not a one-sided gift from God; it also implies a religious pledge on the part of the believer. He must daily earn anew his right to be a 'child of God' by his fulfilment of the Law. The fulfilment is not laid on any one individual, but upon the whole people, irrespective of rank or birth. Hence there is no category of 'saints' as in the Christian Church, officially recognized and accorded canonization by the highest ecclesiastical authorities.

Judaism never took the definitive step towards individual canonization—independent of time, people and place. Thus, even with the dispersion of Jewry, the Holy Land continues to remain the land of the refinement and fulfilment of the Law, the land where God, in the Holy of Holies, entered into direct relation with his people, the land to which the faithful returned again and again through the centuries so as to die in Jerusalem and find their last resting place on the Mount of Olives.

Jewish teaching, the *Torah,* is and always has been a teaching bound up with the idea of a national religion, bound up both with the land and with the Chosen People, and which does not take the step towards the Christian ideal of a universal humanity. Yet it cannot be denied that the prophets, especially Isaiah, have shown distinct tendencies in this direction, but their impetus was insufficient to affect the basic concept of Judaism.

Ye have heard
that it hath been said,
Thou shalt
love thy neighbour,
and hate thine enemy.
But I say unto you,
Love your enemies,
bless them that curse you,
do good to them
that hate you,
and pray for them
which despitefully use you,
and persecute you....

(MATT. 5, 43, 44)

Crucifixion was once the most shameful form of execution in ancient times. The fact that after the death of Christ the cross could become the symbol of suffering and redemption testifies to the fundamental change of outlook brought about by Christianity—after Paul.

Right leaf of bronze door in the abbey church of Bonanus in Monreale near Palermo (1186).

The Jewish people's unbreakable political and religious ties with their country have determined their history: they have kept alive the religious conscience of the individual and of the community, and in the last analysis have preserved them from self-surrender and assimilation into their surroundings. This is the fundamental reason for the survival of the people in their integrity and for their return to their country in the present day.

Blessed are they
that mourn:
for they shall
be comforted.
Blessed are they
which do hunger and thirst
after righteousness:
for they shall be filled.
Blessed are
the pure in heart:
for they shall
see God.
Blessed are
the peacemakers:
for they shall be called
the children of God.
Blessed are they
which are persecuted
for righteousness' sake:
for their's is
the kingdom of heaven.

(MATT. 5, 4, 6, 8–10)

CHRISTIANITY AND PAGANISM

The rise of Christianity cannot be explained in terms of Judaism alone. It has a strong mystical and magical aspect expressed chiefly in the dogma of sacraments such as baptism, the mass, the sacrament of death (Extreme Unction), deriving from late Classical times and having prototypes in the contemporaneous mystery religions.

The early Christian community of Jerusalem, which lived communally and met in 'Solomon's Porch' to the east of the Temple adhered closely to the principles of the Jewish tradition. This early Christian community, whose leaders were the apostles, was compelled to flee to Pella in the Decapolis at the time of the Jewish War (66–70). In this way it lost its spiritual authority which was taken over by the Hellenistic communities. They were communities that had been converted by Paul and consisted of erstwhile Hellenized Jews and erstwhile pagans. Their spiritual centres were in the cosmopolitan cities of the world at that time, Antioch, Alexandria, Ephesus and Rome.

Almost everywhere in those apocalyptically tempestuous times, but especially in the east, mystery cults had arisen whose esoteric rites enabled the initiate to participate in the death and resurrection of the god, thereby securing his personal redemption in an *imitatio dei* (imitation of god).

The deity of the mystery religions, whether he was Tammuz, Adonis, Mithras or Osiris, conformed to the late antique Greek-inspired ideal image of hero and god. His death and resurrection are a symbolic representation of the cosmic cycle. The cultic rites, dramatic and magical in their effects, led the initiate to identify himself with the god, freed him from the self and lifted him above earthly and natural limitations.

CAPTIONS TO COLOUR PLATES

Page 85: The white asphodel, as early as March, decks the hillsides of Israel.

Page 86: The flowering desert.

Page 87: Thistles give their stamp to a stark landscape.

Page 88: Centuries-old olive-tree, landmark of the past.

Christian resurrection, however, is not the resurrection of a god but of a man, Jesus, and his elevation to heaven as the 'Son of God'. The crucifixion and resurrection of Christ are an 'historical' event. While the believer at church mass imitatively experiences Christ's passion and redemption, he experiences the true drama of humanity, but at the same time the certainty of eventual redemption in a divine other world. Pagan man in the mystery religions is 'redeemed' within the circumstances of his existence and of nature. Christian man in a divine kingdom that is absolute and eternal.

With the dogma of the twofold nature of Christ in Pauline Christianity, the foundations of the Church had been laid. Upon these she could continue to build.

THE JEWISH WAR

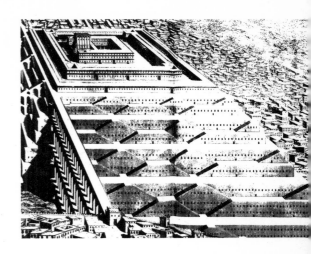

The Jewish War of A.D. 66 to 70 (73) marks the climax of the struggle between the small Jewish nation and the world power of Rome. Although doomed from the start, the effort was rendered immensely more difficult by tragic dissension within the Jewish camp.

The last of the procurators before the outbreak of the war, Gessius Florus (64–66), was also the most ruthless. Driven by an uncontrolled lust for money, he seized seventeen gold talents from the Temple treasure. It was the spark that began a long-threatened conflagration. Rebellion flared up against Rome. The rebels occupied the Temple mountain while the legionaries withdrew into the citadel next to the Temple.

The momentous events that followed—the suspension of the daily sacrifice hitherto made in the Temple in the name of the emperor, the conquest of the mountain fortress of Masada on the Dead Sea by a group of Sicarii and the massacre of its Roman garrison, were tantamount to an open declaration of war on Rome.

When the Roman legionaries in Jerusalem were butchered in spite of their safe-conduct, the Roman governor of Syria, C. Cestius Gallus, found himself compelled to intervene in person. He marched on Jerusalem with his troops, but could not make up his mind to besiege the city. Returning, he fell into a rebel ambush in the Beth-Horon defile from which he only saved himself by fleeing under cover of darkness with heavy losses.

Rome's patience was at an end. The Roman Emperor Nero entrusted Vespasian, the famous general and conqueror of Britain, with the task of crushing the rebellion. In 66 Vespasian assembled an army of three legions and auxiliary forces, altogether some sixty thousand men, in Antioch.

The whole land was now involved in the rebellion. On the day the legionaries were murdered in Jerusalem, the Greek population of Caesarea set upon the Jews. The whole community, no less than twenty thousand, were slaughtered. But in cities where Jews predominated, they fell upon their Gentile neighbours. Retribution was not long in coming, however; according to Josephus, fifty thousand Jews were killed in Alexandria, thirteen thousand in Beth-shean (Scythopolis), two thousand in Ptolemais (Acre) and two thousand four hundred in Joppa (Jaffa).

Vespasian began his offensive, based on Ptolemais, in the spring of 67. It was directed against Galilee which had been put on a defensive footing by Flavius Josephus, who had built up an army and fortified the towns. In spite of this the Jews were not in a position to offer any real resistance to the superior and well-disciplined Roman forces. But the siege of Jotapata, the largest fortified town in Galilee, is a glorious page in the history of this campaign. Under Josephus' command it held out for forty-eight days, falling only as a result of treason (67).

Giscala was the last rebel stronghold in Galilee. But this too was taken by the Romans under Vespasian's son, Titus. The leader of the Jews, Johanan of Giscala, whom Josephus describes as a cunning and unscrupulous rebel, had been able shortly before to fight his way through to Jerusalem with some of his closest followers.

In 20 B.C. Herod I (37–4 B.C.) began his scheme for the reconstruction of the Jerusalem Temple, regarding as unworthy of so fine a city as Jerusalem the modest Temple built by Zerubbabel (515). It was not until A.D. 64 that the third Temple, one of the largest sacred places known in antiquity, was completed under Herod Agrippa II, six years before its destruction. The Temple of Herod was the sanctuary which Christ knew.

Reconstruction of the Temple precincts (after Bernard Lamy, 1720).

T. Flavius Vespasian, the commander in the Roman war against Judea, was Roman Emperor from A.D. 69 to 79. He had been in the country since 66, and had successfully put down the Jewish insurrection of 66–70. He had bronze *Judaea Capta* coins struck, showing a lamenting female figure and a fettered warrior, with the inscription: *Imp(erator) Caes(ar) Vespasian Aug(ustus) — Judaea capta* (Judea conquered).

Flavius Josephus (A.D. 37–c. 100), belonged to a distinguished Jewish family of priests in Jerusalem. On the outbreak of the revolt against the Romans (66) he was leader and organizer of the rebels in Galilee, was taken prisoner by the Romans after the fall of Jotapata (67), but was released in 69, having won the favour of Vespasian. He was an intermediary during the siege of Jerusalem by Titus (70) and witnessed the destruction of the city and of the Temple. Josephus, famous as the most important Jewish historian, has left us a vivid account of the dramatic events of that epoch in his vast work *The Jewish War*.

Wood engraving (eighteenth century).

When Jerusalem fell in A.D. 70, Vespasian's elder son, Titus, tried in vain to prevent the Temple from being burnt down. After Titus' death in 81, a triumphal arch was raised in his honour in Rome, the inside of which has two reliefs depicting the triumph after the capture of Jerusalem. Our picture shows the seven-branched candelabrum belonging to the Temple treasure borne in the triumphal procession.

There he became the leader of the Zealots, first allying himself with the moderate party in Jerusalem, only to betray their plans to the Zealots. The latter, feeling insecure in relation to the great mass of the people, at Johanan's instigation called on the Idumeans for help, thereby unleashing a civil war in which thousands were killed and in the process initiating a veritable reign of terror.

Then an opponent appeared in the person of Simon bar Giora. This chieftain from Idumea was a man of radical democratic ideas and decreed the emancipation of slaves in districts under his rule. Soon he had gathered fifteen thousand men with Masada, held by the Sicarii, as his base. The moderate party itself opened the doors of Jerusalem to him in the belief that he would prove an ally. It was a dire mistake—Simon bar Giora fought them as he fought the Zealots. In consequence the town was ruled by two gangs, each fighting the other and each terrorizing the rest of the inhabitants. One of the acts of folly in this triangular civil war was the burning of the grain stores.

Vespasian's generals were pressing for a siege of Jerusalem. He, however, preferred to subdue the whole country first. When he had achieved this, by the summer of 68, the political situation in Rome had changed fundamentally. Nero had committed suicide. Vespasian, summoned by the legions to be Caesar, left the country for Rome. He left the siege of Jerusalem to his son, and in the spring of 70 Titus marched against the city with an army of sixty-five thousand soldiers. In face of the common danger, the different hostile groups in the city united.

The besiegers at first suffered considerable losses since the Jews were making almost continuous sallies and fought with the courage of desperation. Several times they succeeded in destroying the heavy siege engines of the Romans. Jerusalem was protected by three strong walls. There were almost impregnable bulwarks in the forum of the Temple, and the Antonia fortress in the east of the city, Herod's palace with its three towers, Phasael, Hippicus and Mariamne in the west.

The siege lasted nearly five months. The last to fall were the Temple and Herod's palace. Titus was ready to spare the Temple and offered the rebels safe-conduct. The suggestion was turned down with contumely, although the rebels were at the point of starvation. The Temple was taken by storm and went up in flames.

The town fell at the end of August 70 A.D. It was again the 9th Ab, the national day of ill omen for the people, the day on which the first Temple had fallen. Jerusalem was razed to the ground. The only things left standing were part of the city wall and Herod's palace with its three mighty towers.

Of the thousands of prisoners, seven hundred were taken for the triumph in Rome. The splendour of the victory celebrations is still visible today in Titus' triumphal arch. All the booty of the war was put on show, including the seven-branched candelabrum of the Temple and its gold and silver utensils. The high point of the triumph was the execution of Simon bar Giora in the Forum.

Only three fortresses of Herod's time still held out in the country; these were Herodium, Machaerus and Masada. For three long years Masada, the precipitous mountain fortress above the Dead Sea, was defended by nine hundred men. Freedom-loving and proud, they took their own lives when there was no more room for hope. Potsherds with the names of defenders, which were found among the rubble of the razed fortress, were probably used for casting lots to determine the order of death.

The defeat sealed the fate of the Jewish state. But not the fate of the Jewish people. While the siege of Jerusalem was still in progress, Johanan ben Zakkai in his wisdom and foresight had obtained permission from Titus to start a new house of learning at Jamnia, not far from the sea south of Joppa. Legend has it that he reached Titus by having himself carried through the Roman lines in a coffin by his pupils. Soon after the war, most of the surviving scholars and rabbis gathered at Jamnia.

Sacrificial service had ceased with the destruction of the Temple, and the priestly party, the Sadducees, no longer existed. The scriptural scholarship of the rabbis, represented by the party of the Pharisees, was from this time the only spiritual authority the people possessed. In the communities, the place of the Temple was taken by the house of learning and the synagogue.

The judicial and administrative council, the Sanhedrin, was restored. At its head was the *Nassi*, or prince, also called Patriarch, whose office was hereditary. The Patriarchate, officially recognized by Rome in the second century, afforded new spiritual leadership both to communities within the country and to those of the *diaspora*.

The most famous of the Patriarchs, Judah ha-Nassi, was responsible for systematically collecting and recording the post-exilic, oral traditional doctrine of Judaism, the *Mishnah*.

In the ensuing centuries, from the third to the fifth, discussions in the religious schools gave rise to a sentence-by-sentence commentary on the Mishnah, and this was set down in the *Gemara*. Mishnah and Gemara are the twin pillars of the Talmud.

The Talmud exists in two versions; the Palestinian and the Babylonian. The much more comprehensive Babylonian Talmud, completed out in the fifth century, was the one upon which the social, legal and religious life of the Jews was chiefly based. It is the sequel to the Torah, or Biblical teaching, adapting it to contemporary historical conditions up to the present day. For the next two thousand years it was to ensure the survival of Judaism in its own characteristic form, after what was probably its severest crisis, the Jewish War.

Even though the national sovereignty of the people was broken, its spiritual and religious independence had survived intact. Even though the walls of Jerusalem had fallen, the bastions of the Law still guarded Judaism, and they had not been shaken.

The mass suicide of rebellious Jews beleaguered in the fortress of Masada (A.D. 73) —there were more than nine hundred men, women and children—is unique in the history of mankind. It became the symbol of the Jewish people's deep-rooted love of freedom.
Imaginary picture of the siege (1692).

BAR-COCHBA'S REBELLION

In the rebellions of the centuries that followed, the Jewish people's unbroken will to live was manifested; it was sustained by the hope of the imminent appearance of the Messiah. Every new uprising that broke out had not only the political aim of shaking off Roman rule, but was also seen as the final religious war before the coming of the Messiah.

There is no historian of the calibre of Flavius Josephus to tell us about the times that followed. We know very little about the rebellions in the *diaspora* in 115, at the time of the emperor Trajan, which spread from Cyrene and Alexandria to Cyprus and even as far as Mesopotamia, and which were crushed with unbelievable harshness by Rome.

But the rebellion of 132–5 was restricted to Judea. Its immediate cause appears to have been Hadrian's edict forbidding circumcision and the practice of the cult under pain of death, and the order to rebuild Jerusalem as a Roman colony, Aelia Capitolina, where the Temple destroyed by Titus was to be replaced by a pagan temple. Simeon ben Kosiba became leader of the rebellion; he was known to his followers as Bar-Cochba (son of the stars). Recognized as Messiah by the Rabbi Akiba, the venerable and famous scholar, Bar-Cochba had a tremendous following and great success in war. The Romans were virtually driven out of the country and Jerusalem appears to have been recaptured and held for two years. This is borne out by Bar-

Simeon Bar-Cochba, who led the last great revolt of the Jews against the Romans (A.D. 132–35), during the few years of his leadership had bronze and silver coins struck with designs that symbolized the aim of the rebellion: the reconstruction of the Temple as a sign of the freedom of Judea. The inscriptions are

in ancient Hebrew script, which had hardly been used since the introduction of Aramaic characters after the Babylonian captivity.
Inscription on the reverse side of a small silver coin: *Lecherut Jeruschalem* ('To the freedom of Jerusalem').

Coin of the Emperor Hadrian (A.D. 117–38), probably minted just before the outbreak of the Jewish revolt under Bar-Cochba (132).
Inscription: *Hadrianus Augustus*.

Cochba coins with the inscription 'Simeon, Prince of Israel, 1 (and 2) year of the liberation of Israel', and 'To the freedom of Jerusalem'.

The rebellion, which developed into ferocious guerilla warfare, was carried on by the Jews from inaccessible caves in the mountains round the Dead Sea. Even Hadrian's great general, Julius Severus, had no means of subduing the rebels except starvation.

Bar-Cochba fell in 135, at the place of his last stand, Bethar, the mountain fortress near Jerusalem. According to tradition, it was again the 9th Ab, the day of national disaster Judea was almost depopulated. The survivors took refuge in the mountains of Galilee, where a new centre of Judaism arose.

After the war was over, Jerusalem was rebuilt as a Roman provincial city, Colonia Aelia Capitolina. In place of the Jewish Temple, a heathen one was erected and dedicated to Jupiter Capitolinus. Jews were forbidden under pain of death to enter their city. And even the name of the province, Judea, was regarded as too reminiscent of the 'Land of the Jews', so that it was henceforward known as Palestine.

Judaism would almost certainly have died out altogether but for the mitigation of Hadrian's anti-religious measures under his successor, Antoninus Pius.

It was indeed their active opposition to Rome that earned for the Jews recognition as a national and religious minority. With Caracalla's edict of 212 they became fully enfranchised Roman citizens, though they still had to pay a special tax, the *fiscus Judaicus*. The Christian communities, on the other hand, were subject to Roman law and, because they refused to sacrifice to the statues of the gods or to the deified Caesar, they were repeatedly and mercilessly persecuted. After the first limited operations under Nero (64), Domitian (81–96) and Trajan (98–117), Christians were systematically persecuted under Decius (249–51) and Diocletian (303–11), when thousands died as martyrs.

Under Constantine the Great the position changed. In 313 he granted Christianity throughout the empire full and equal rights alongside the old, heathen cults, going out of his way, indeed, to favour the Christian communities. Only two years later, the first anti-Jewish decrees were promulgated. Having come to power, the oppressed became in their turn oppressors. Thus began the tragic history of medieval and modern Jewry, starting in the Byzantine (East Roman) empire and in the countries of Europe. The more secure the position of the Church, whether in East Rome or West Rome, the more she combatted Judaism, to which she owed her origins. Whereas both religions at the beginning of the fourth century still had much in common, the efforts of the church Fathers and the ecclesiastical policy of the Byzantine state concentrated increasingly on emphasizing the differences. The Council of Nicaea laid down so rigid a calendar of festivals that there was no longer any chance of confusion with that of Judaism. Marriages between Christians and Jews were forbidden under pain of death. Jews were not allowed to keep Christian—and later pagan—slaves. Attempts at conversion were punished with death, and this applied equally to convert and converter. In 425 Theodosius II abolished the office of Patriarch and excluded Jews from holding public office. It was a severe blow for Palestinian Jewry, for it was thus condemned to insignificance. The rise of Christianity in the Byzantine empire brought about the political disenfranchisement of the Jews and their social ostracism. They became the pawn of religious fanaticism and of political caprice.

By contrast, under Islam in Mesopotamia and in Spain new centres arose where Jewish spiritual life could flourish.

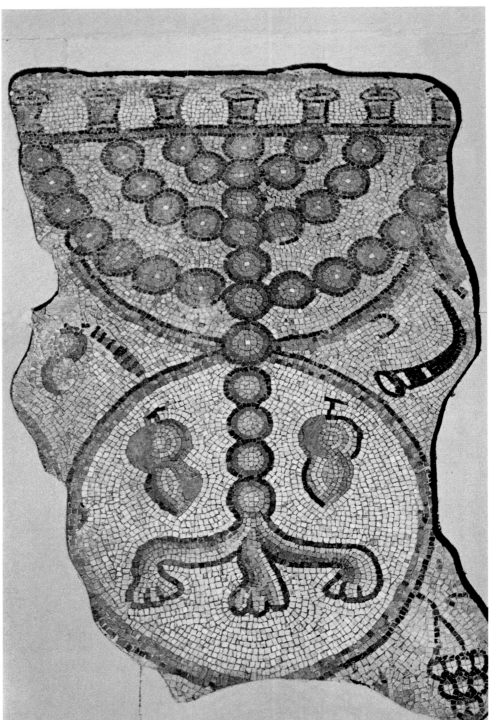

MESOPOTAMIAN JEWRY

Moses holding the Book of the Law (detail). Wall-painting in the Dura-Europos Synagogue (*c.* A.D. 200).

Mesopotamian Jewry could look back over a long history. Its ancestors were those who had remained in Babylon and whose communities described themselves as *Golah* (exile). The spiritual bond was maintained with the land of their fathers by annual pilgrimages to Jerusalem and the payment of the usual Temple tribute.

The history of this Jewish centre in Mesopotamia, which was ruled first by the Persians and then by the Parthians until A.D. 224, is for several centuries veiled in darkness. Only from the second century A.D. do we hear anything of its secular leader, the Exilarch, who resided in Babylon and held a court of princely splendour. His legal status was largely recognized by the rulers of the country, and he collected on their behalf the high taxes imposed upon the Jews. In return, the Golah was granted autonomy and its own judiciary. The centres of Jewish life were Nehardea, Sura, Mahoza and Pumbeditha—all seats of a high flowering of civilization and culture.

During the rule of the New Persian kingdom of the Sassanids (224–651), the Jewish communities' rights of self-government were restricted, and the Jews suffered from persecution by Zoroastrian priests. Yet during this time Mesopotamian Jewry made a permanent contribution to Jewish spiritual life. In the religious academies of Nehardea, Sura, Mahoza and Pumbeditha, the foundations of the Babylonian Talmud were laid.

With the conquest of the Near East by Arabian tribes after 633 the position of the Golah, which had suffered from a policy of oppression and religious hatred, changed. In A.D. 634 the great Caliph Omar had recognized the Exilarch, and under the tolerance of the Islamic caliphs, the Baghdad Exilarchate achieved its greatest brilliance. Never had the heads of the two leading academies of Sura and Pumbeditha, now called Geonim, attained to such authority as they did now, during the epoch of the Arabian world kingdom. Their decisions, the *Responsa*, in all questions of Bible and Talmud interpretation, of liturgy and jurisdiction, were uncontested throughout world Jewry.

From amongst the ranks of the Jews themselves there arose after the eighth century the movement of the Karaites, running counter to traditional rabbinic Judaism; it recognized only the Bible and rejected the Talmud. Everywhere from Persia to Spain, the sect won great support, and finally threatened to oust rabbinic Judaism. It was saved by Saadiah ben Joseph, president of the academy of Sura since 928 and the most important of the Geonim. Many of his writings show that the religious tradition set down in the Talmud is an organic continuation of the Bible. Thus he became the founder of a new form of Biblical interpretation and of a systematic philosophical outlook upon which all later Jewish philosophy was built.

The flowering of Mesopotamian Jewry lasted into the eleventh century. The academies progressively lost their authority to the newly founded schools in Spain, North Africa and Europe, and the conquest and destruction of Baghdad by the Mongols in 1258 brought the Exilarchate to an end.

Considerable light was shed on the high level of culture of Mesopotamian Jewry by the discovery of the Dura-Europos Synagogue on the middle Euphrates. Dura-Europos was a fortress which was founded by the Seleucids at the beginning of the third century, fell into the hands of the Parthians in 100 B.C., into those of the Romans in A.D. 165 and was taken and destroyed by the Persians in 256. Excavations laid bare the ruins of a synagogue built about A.D. 200; it is decorated with impressive frescos of Old Testament subjects, which seem to foreshadow early Christian and Byzantine art.

The completion of the Babylonian Talmud in the fifth century A.D. which, together with the Jerusalem Talmud, formed the basis for the conduct of the whole of Jewry in the Middle Ages and in modern times, must be regarded as the crowning achievement of the tremendous exegetic work carried out by the Mesopotamian academies. The decline of the Palestinian Patriarchate under Byzantine overlordship in the fourth and fifth centuries brought about the transference of Jewish leadership to the schools of Mesopotamia.

Great is the Lord,
and greatly to be praised
in the city
of our God,
in the mountain
of his holiness.

(PSALM 48, 1)

JERUSALEM, CITY OF THREE RELIGIONS

David's Tower to the west of the present Old City, a landmark in Jerusalem, is the minaret of a mosque belonging to the medieval citadel which was built on the vast remains of Herod's palace.

Silver tetradrachm of Simeon Bar-Cochba, between A.D. 132–135. Inscription: Simeon. Between the two central columns of the Temple is the Ark of the Covenant. The star above the façade is probably the Messianic symbol of Bar-Cochba, the Son of the Star.

In the history of mankind, cities are centres where economic, cultural and political powers are concentrated. The peculiarity of Jerusalem was that it also grew into a religious centre, and as such attained world-wide significance.

Ever since David's conquest of the city and the erection of the Temple on Mount Moriah by Solomon, Jerusalem had been the focal point of the people's religious and political life.

Set high up in the mountains of Judea away from the caravan routes, city and sanctuary became the object of three national pilgrimages a year; in the spring at the time of the Passover, in the summer for the Feast of the Weeks (Shavuoth) and in autumn for the harvest festival (Sukkoth).

The Temple was God's place of meeting with his people. When the people set out for Jerusalem, therefore, their journey was a symbolic approach to God, the way to an inner purging (*catharsis*) and the way to a constantly renewed covenant with God.

God's omnipresence and the covenant made with his people represent the basic religious concepts of Judaism. They are confirmed in the daily actions of the individual, a perpetual 'dialogue' with his God.

On the other hand, God is unapproachable, removed far above and outside his creation. The Jewish God is thus at one and the same time a transcendent and an immanent God who, in spite of his distant elevation is always and everywhere present and active. Man, therefore, in the course of history, fulfills the divine plan which is to work towards the Messianic era and to achieve the kingdom of God on earth. But Jerusalem, the mountain city, is destined at the end of time to gather her children about her and to lead mankind to redemption.

The religious and cultic significance of Jerusalem has found frequent expression in poetic and mythical images in the Psalms and the prophetic books. In Ezekiel the city (or the Temple) is called the world's navel, a magic and religious concept which later on—in Flavius Josephus and in Philo of Alexandria—was fairly common. In medieval maps and up till modern times, Jerusalem is always the centre of the world.

Even when Jewish political independence had become a thing of the past, in A.D. 70, Jerusalem continued to be the religious centre of the Jewish people of the dispersion. Thus, in an astonishing way, the city preserved the religious and national spirit of Jewry throughout the centuries, and lies at the very foundation of present-day political Zionism.

For Christendom, spreading ever further, Jerusalem still remained the heart of the new world-religion, even though by this time its oecumenical centres were in Rome, with the Pope, and in Byzantium (Constantinople) with the Byzantine emperor and the Patriarch.

The new eschatological teaching of Christianity was rooted in Jerusalem and was a continuation of the doctrine of Judaism, whereas Christian mysticism, revelation and transcendence ran counter to the Jewish tradition. Jesus sees Jerusalem as the scene of his mission. As a believing Jew, he and his disciples go there for the Passover. The city is the scene of his passion and his death on the cross. But it is also the scene of the miracle of Christ's resurrection by which he is redeemed from death, from suffering and all earthly insufficiency, being elevated to a world that is absolute and everlasting. He becomes the mediator between the perfect, heavenly world of God·and the material world enmeshed in original sin.

The Judaistic doctrine of the One (monotheism) was thus disrupted through the agency of Paul, by a new, dualistic Persian doctrine, upon which the first foundations of the eschatological dogma of the Church were laid.

The Christian dualistic view of the world has been of immense import in the history of mankind. Its conception of the other world, a pale abstraction, acquired a visionary life from the poetic and legendary images with which it became overlaid. The other world and eternity are portrayed in the form of a shining city surrounded by towers. The Joannine Revelation, in particular, describes the vision of the heavenly city in glowing terms:

> And I John saw the holy city, new Jerusalem, coming down from God out of heaven, prepared as a bride adorned for her husband. And I heard a great voice out of heaven saying, Behold, the tabernacle of God is with men, and he will dwell with them, and they shall be his people, and God himself shall be with them, and be their God.
> (REV. 21, 2–3)

The entire religious development of the Middle Ages, whether it be liturgy, church architecture or any of the arts connected with the church, took place under the spell of these visionary images.

Church architecture, especially that of the cathedrals, represents a bold attempt to realize the heavenly Jerusalem here on earth. The most important cultic centre of Christendom, the Church of the Holy Sepulchre built by Constantine the Great in Jerusalem, is described as the 'New Jerusalem'. He also built the Constantinian basilica and the rotunda of the Holy Sepulchre. Between these, in the atrium, there is Golgotha and immediately next to it, marked by the presence of a stone basin, the 'navel of the world'.

The Church of the Middle Ages was seen by Christians as the 'New Temple', the choir being 'the throne of God'. At the same time, like the Church of the Holy Sepulchre, it represents the new and heavenly Jerusalem, a view reflected in many literary and religious documents.

Such eschatological ideas are realized in different ways at different times. Whereas in the early Christian era the church building—like the Church of the Holy Sepulchre —represents a kind of urban architecture, Byzantine in character, during the Romanesque period in the eleventh and twelfth centuries it becomes defensive, rather resembling a fortress. Later, in Gothic times, cathedrals attained the most perfect architectural realization of visionary transcendental ideas in the glowing colours of stained glass, in the infinite, upthrusting dynamic of compound columns and buttresses, and in the immateriality of walls.

The liturgy that takes place within this framework also expresses religious, eschatological concepts. The mass is its heart and its head. Originally an imitative repetition of Jesus' Passover meal in Jerusalem, it becomes in Jesus' mystical presence a magical and religious act. His words when breaking bread: 'This is my body', and in drinking the wine: 'This is my blood' have become the sacramental words of

... for the law
shall go forth
of Zion, and the word
of the Lord
from Jerusalem.

(MICAH 4, 2)

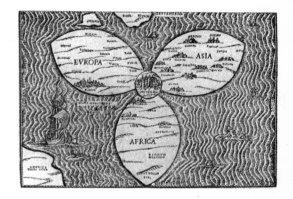

Map of the world, dated 1585. Diagrammatic presentation of the continents of Europe, Asia and Africa in the shape of three congruent, ovaloid figures with Jerusalem at their centre.

The Heavenly Jerusalem. Woodcut by Lucas Cranach, from the first edition of Luther's Bible (1534).

The ascent to heaven of gods and heroes is a universal and timeless motif in legend. One tells how Mohammed, on the she-ass Buraq, with veiled face and surrounded by an aureole, was accompanied to the Seventh Heaven by the Archangel Gabriel. The ascent is said to have taken place from Mount Moriah; this is the only religious subject found in Islamic book illumination (1502).

the mass which conjure up the presence of Christ. The believer, in eating the bread (Host) and drinking the wine, incorporates Christ within himself and experiences in an *imitatio dei*, an inner purification and redemption.

In contrast to the Jewish conception of an immanent, omnipresent God with whom the individual is in a constant relation of dialogue, the Christian, transcendental God is 'conjured up' by means of a mystical-magical act. In contrast to the individual responsibility of action of the Jew, who is enabled at any time to communicate directly with his God, the 'redemption' of the Christian becomes an 'act of grace' of the absolute, unconditioned God.

In the dualistic Christian view of the world, the distance between the material world enmeshed in original sin and the perfection of the divine world is virtually unbridgable. Thus it requires a whole army of 'saints' and 'Servants of God', beginning with Christ, to form a kind of intermediate realm between heaven and the earthly vale of woe. This 'halfway' realm mediates between the two spheres and is a guarantee of eventual redemption for the believer. The Christian Church's cult of saints has become an important part of the believer's religious life.

Cultural development in medieval Europe took place wholly within the Church. It was a development of vast dimensions in which all the creative faculties of man were engaged—in architecture, in painting and sculpture, in music and poetry, in liturgy and cult. It was creation *sub specie aeternitatis*—designed to reassure man as to his eventual redemption in a vision of eternity. With it, the foundations of European culture and civilization were laid. That the 'heavenly Jerusalem' formed the setting for this emphasizes the historical role of the eternal city. It is equally the symbolic expression of the tremendous contribution of Judaism and Christianity to the history of mankind.

CAPTIONS TO COLOUR PLATES

Page 105: On Mount Moriah where once the Temple stood, the cupola of the Dome of the Rock towers above the walls and houses of Old Jerusalem. The Dome of the Rock is the oldest Moslem monumental building in the Near East, built in A.D. 691 by the Caliph Abd el-Malik of the dynasty of the Ommayads.

Pages 106/107: Above the East wall of the former temple, rebuilt by Sultan Suleiman the Magnificent (1520–66), the houses of the Old City, recently reunited with the new town of Jerusalem, rise steeply. The two arches in the wall—remains of the Byzantine era—mark the position of the 'Golden Gate' through which, according to an old legend, the Messiah would enter. The Jews called it 'Gate of Mercy' and prayed there for the Temple to be rebuilt.

Page 108: Overarched by buttresses and lined with small shops and workshops, the Via Dolorosa is a typical stepped alleyway in Old Jerusalem, and is both street and market.

Mohammed's original intention to make Judaism's venerable religious centre that of the new faith was thwarted by the refusal, contrary to his hopes, of the Jews in Arabia, and especially those of Medina, to go over to Islam, and a veritable war of persecution began as a result of which many Jewish communities in the peninsula lost their homes. This induced Mohammed to decide that his own native town, Mecca, should be the cultic centre of the new doctrine. However, *El Kuds* (the holy one)—Jerusalem—still remained the third holy city of Islam, after Mecca and Medina.

Under the Caliph Abd el-Malik an attempt was made, by building the Dome of the Rock in 691 on the site of the former Temple, to transfer the centre from Mecca to Jerusalem. The attempt failed, but Abd el-Malik was the first to build an Islamic sanctuary of monumental proportions and was the founder of Islamic art in general.

In the Arab legend, Mount Moriah, on which the Temple stood and upon which the Dome of the Rock was built, was Mohammed's place of departure for his *miraj*, the prophet's ascent by night to the Seventh Heaven on his ass Buraq.

It is typical of Islamic doctrine that the prophet's *miraj* took place during his lifetime and not after death, and that its location was Mount Moriah. For Islam, too, Jerusalem is the mountain city, a neighbour of the heavenly regions.

Today Jerusalem is the capital of the state of Israel. And in spite of politics she still remains, as she has been for centuries, the holy city of three religions.

IN THE SHADOW OF THE CRUSADES

What a wondrous and lovely spectacle were for us all those gleaming crosses of silk, gold or other kind of cloth sewn by the pilgrims at the Pope's behest to the back of their cloaks, robes or tunics! (Fulcher of Chartres).

Crusaders on their way to the Holy Land (fourteenth century book illustration).

Constantine the Great's edict of toleration in 313 marked the definitive victory of Christianity. After violent disputes concerning the orthodoxy of imperial church doctrine, the decisions were left in the hands of the Councils of Nicaea (325) and of Constantinople (381): Christianity, proclaimed the only religion of the state, became the third pillar of the empire together with the army and the public service. Roman in law and government, Greek as to language and culture, Christian as to faith and morality, the Byzantine empire laid the foundations for the christianization of Europe.

The attraction of the Holy Land for the faithful, and especially of Jerusalem, the scene of Christ's passion, soon brought in an unending stream of pilgrims, the more so after Constantine the Great had built those great sanctuaries of Christendom, the Church of the Holy Sepulchre in Jerusalem and the Church of the Nativity in Bethlehem.

As a result of this abundant and perennial flow of pilgrims into the country there were large-scale church and monastic building operations, and it is reported that at the beginning of the fifth century more than three hundred monasteries existed in Jerusalem alone, affording accommodation for pilgrims and hospitals for the sick.

Over and above this there was a wealth of spiritual activity which manifested itself in the works of the Early Fathers, such as Origen and Eusebius, and in Jerome's Latin translation of the Bible, the Vulgate.

All this activity ceased abruptly with the wave of Arab conquest which engulfed a large part of the Byzantine empire and within a few decades had deprived it of whole regions such as Syria, Palestine, Egypt and North Africa.

With the spread of the Arabs throughout the Near East and round the shores of the Mediterranean, there could no longer be the same intensive commerce as had existed earlier between those countries and Europe. Travel by sea or by land became hazardous since the routes were haunted by pirates and robbers.

In these circumstances, when pilgrimages entailed so great a risk to life and property, they virtually ceased. They were not resumed until the eighth and ninth centuries, with the cordial relations established with the Caliph Harun al-Rashid by Charlemagne. At the end of the eighth century, the caliph handed over the keys of the Church of the Holy Sepulchre at Aix and recognized a Frankish protectorate over the holy places.

When in the tenth century the Byzantine empire had recovered some of her strength, pilgrimages also revived and during the eleventh century assumed considerable proportions.

During the tenth and eleventh centuries, Palestine was subject to the rule of the Egyptian Fatimid dynasty whose attitude towards the Christian pilgrims was on the whole one of tolerance. An exception was the half-insane el-Hakim who persecuted Christians, Jews and even Moslems indiscriminately and caused the Church of the Holy Sepulchre and many other churches to be demolished.

This figurehead of a 'Good Shepherd' found in Acre must have adorned the prow of a pilgrim ship. The style is Gothic, but the piece belongs to the nineteenth century approximately, for such figureheads were unknown in the Middle Ages.

Sultan Saladin, the great antagonist of the Crusaders, was of Kurdish descent. He was the founder of the Ayyubid dynasty (1171–1250), which succeeded the Fatimids in 1171. He was able to unite Egypt, Syria and Mesopotamia under his rule and to drive the Crusaders out of the land in 1187, after the Battle of Hattin and the fall of Jerusalem.

Persian miniature (twelfth century).

Richard I, Cœur-de-Lion (1189–99), king of England, was the leader of the Third Crusade. Together with Philip II Augustus, king of France, he re-captured Acre in 1191, thus securing the territory between Tyre and Ashkelon—with the exception of Jerusalem—for the Frankish Kingdom. His often cruel methods of warfare compared unfavourably with those of his magnanimous opponent, Saladin.

Book illustration: Surrender of the city of Acre to King Philip and King Richard Cœur-de-Lion (left).

The situation changed completely with the arrival in 1071 of the Turkish Seljuks in Asia Minor, Syria and Palestine. The eleventh and twelfth centuries were characterized by the victorious campaigns of these and related Turkish tribes in the Near East. After the decisive Battle of Manzikert in 1071 almost the whole of Asia Minor was in their hands and the Byzantine empire was immediately threatened.

The gradual advance of these nomad peoples from Central Asia had begun in the seventh century A.D. In the tenth century they accepted Islam and with the conquest of Baghdad (1055) they became the mainstay of the caliphate which had fallen into rapid decline. Perpetually at war with Constantinople, they succeeded in consolidating themselves in Asia Minor and in founding a large number of emirates, the most important being the Seljuk kingdom of Rum with its capital at Konia (Iconium).

In Syria and Palestine the Seljuks clashed with the Fatimids by whom their victorious advance was soon brought to a halt.

The threat to Constantinople, the almost total interruption of pilgrimages by the raids of the Seljuks, and the desecration of the holy places were the immediate cause of the Crusades. Pope Urban II's call at the Council of Clermont in 1095 to free the holy places awoke a tremendous response. In fiery sermons, preachers spread the idea of the Crusades and soon not only in addition to the regular levies of the knights but wholesale population movements were making their way towards the Holy Land, only to come to a pitiful end in Hungary.

The crusading enthusiasm had catastrophic results for the many Jewish communities in the Rhineland, in France, in Bavaria and in Bohemia. The hatred of 'unbelievers' was directed in the first place against those who were at hand—the Jews, who were generally held to have crucified Jesus. Under the leadership of the Count Emico von Leiningen the mass of people, mostly peasants, who had pledged their services to the Crusades, were set on to attack the Jewish communities of Metz, Spires, Mainz, Worms, Cologne and other towns. In many places authorities and prelates did all they could to protect the Jews, but against the mob they were powerless. The community at Worms was wiped out almost to the last man. About five hundred had taken refuge from their pursuers in the episcopal palace; a week later the building was surrounded and, in spite of the bishop's protests, the Jews were murdered.

The crusading army of knights reached Constantinople towards the end of 1096, and in April 1097 they crossed the Bosphorus with Jerusalem as their goal. In Asia Minor they first encountered, and learned to respect, their Turkish enemy. After heavy and bloody fighting they reached Antioch in October of the same year. This, the largest city of the Near East, was an almost impregnable fortress commanding communications to the north, east and south. After a seven months' siege, on 3 June 1098, a traitor delivered up the town to the enemy.

It was a year before the main body of troops under Godefroi de Bouillon had reached Jerusalem, although they had not stopped on the way to beleaguer and take fortified towns, such as Acre. Wells round Jerusalem were poisoned, the surrounding country laid waste. The armies suffered from the summer heat and they were hungry and thirsty. The whole complement of the army—twelve hundred knights and twelve thousand foot-soldiers—was too small to surround the city, which remained open on the south side.

But with the help of specially built strong siege towers Jerusalem was stormed on 15 July 1099. An appalling bloodbath ensued among Moslems and Jews. The Jews took refuge in their largest synagogue; it was set on fire, and all perished in the flames. That was the end of the Jewish community in Jerusalem.

The first half of the twelfth century was devoted to consolidating the Crusaders' kingdom and incorporating into it those towns not previously occupied. In the second half of the century, Saladin, the famous opponent of the Crusaders, was able to reunite Egypt and Syria. In 1187, after the decisive Battle of Hattin near Tiberias, and after the fall of Jerusalem, Acre and most of the other cities, practically every Crusader was driven out of the country, and their political sovereignty came to an end.

The answer of European Christendom to this desperate situation was the Third Crusade (1189–93). It was conducted by the three kings, Richard I Cœur de Lion of England, Philipp II Augustus of France and Frederick I Barbarossa of the Holy Roman Empire.

Again there were persecutions of the Jews, which this time spread to England. In York there was a virtual siege of the community which had taken refuge in the Keep. When there was no longer hope of rescue they died at one another's hands.

The Third Crusade saved the Frankish kingdom. Acre was recaptured by Richard Cœur-de-Lion and Philip Augustus and for exactly a hundred years was to stay the capital of what remained of the kingdom; this was confined largely to the coastal towns of Antioch, Tortosa, Tripoli, Beirut, Sidon, Tyre, Acre, Caesarea and Jaffa. The Crusaders never succeeded in recapturing Jerusalem, in spite of several attempts like the one led by Richard Cœur-de-Lion.

An extremely rare combination of the lion of St. Mark and the eagle of St. John in a style unusually dramatic for the thirteenth century (sandstone), forming the decoration of a pulpit.

SPANISH JEWRY

In A.D. 711, the Arabs under their leader Tarik crossed the Straits of Gibraltar and entered Spain where they were greeted by the Jews as liberators. Within four years the conquerors had extended their dominion as far as the Pyrenees. With Cordova as the seat of the caliphate, there ensued a brilliant cultural flowering in which the Jews played a prominent part. While Europe was still slowly recovering from the effects of the migrations of the nations, there grew up in Spain a new intellectual world upon which Europe was later able to build.

Spanish Jews were free and equal citizens with a right to their own jurisdiction and they were active in all walks of life and all occupations, whether that of Vizier or ambassador, doctor or astronomer, philosopher or poet, that of farmer or craftsman or soldier, wealthy merchant or tax farmer or money-lender. Trade with the east was largely in their hands, since Christian merchants were at great risk in Moslem countries. Very probably the regular contact with Jewish centres of learning in Mesopotamia and Palestine was maintained through these merchants. After the demise of the Mesopotamian schools of Sura and Pumbeditha, Cordova inherited their great intellectual tradition.

Jewish scholars were inspired by the flourishing state of Arab science and literature and a spate of translations ensued. Arab translations of Aristotle were put into Hebrew and from this into Latin by Jewish scholars from Provence. In this way Aristotle became known to the intellectual world of Europe at its awakening, a factor of incalculable importance in the history of culture.

One of the first scholars we know of is Hasdai ibn Shaprut (c. 915–70), court physician to Abd-er-Rahman III and to his successor Hakam II. Thanks to his good knowledge

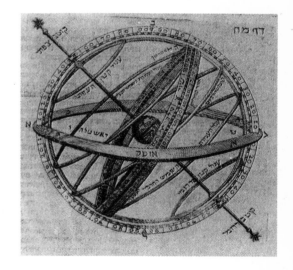

Spanish Jewry produced not only physicians, scientists and philosophers of note, but also furthered the theoretical and practical development of astronomy. The Jews' special skill as cartographers and constructors of astrolabes frequently led to their participation in the preparation and execution of voyages of discovery to India and America. Thus Vasco da Gama's adviser was the well-known Jewish astronomer Abraham Zacuto.

Astrolabe with Hebrew lettering (1707).

OF HUMILITY
OF HUMILITY
(Part I, Chapter 2)

It is related of an illustrious king,
that one night while a number of
people were assembled about him,
he arose to trim the lamp. Whereupon
it was said to him, 'Why didst thou not
utter a command, which would have
sufficed?' And he answered them,
'As a king I rose, and as a king I resume
my seat.'... Humility is the only quality
which no man envies. When one is gifted
with its presence, he has already
gained superiority. It is said,
'Whomsoever the Lord loveth he
inspireth with contentment.'

From the *Improvement of the Moral Qualities*
by Solomon ibn Gabirol. The Spanish Jew and
poet-philosopher of the eleventh century had a
great influence on Christian theology of the
Middle Ages through his principal work
Source of Life.

of Latin, he was entrusted with many diplomatic missions, especially to the Christian courts in northern Spain. He carried them out with great skill, and in recognition of his services was appointed Intendant General of Customs in Cordova.

Hasdai was also a generous patron of science. Such was the influence of this exceptional man that Talmudic scholarship found a new home in Spain and Cordova became the Andalusian Sura.

Nor was he forgetful of his own people. He was able through diplomatic channels to help many Jewish communities of the *diaspora* in time of need and to protect them against persecution and oppression.

Samuel the Nagid (993–1063) is an example of a Spanish Jew whose intellectual qualities raised him from obscurity to fame and splendour. Starting as a small grocer, he became King's Vizier in Granada where he served twenty-five years, and Nassi (prince) of the Jews. He was poet, scholar and statesman and on occasion personally led forces in the field. He was, too, a tireless Maecenas and the great library which he had built in his residence in Granada contained valuable treasures.

One of the many poets and philosophers of whom he was the patron was Solomon ibn Gabirol (c. 1021–69), whose deeply sincere liturgical songs are still used today in the Sephardic synagogue services. Ibn Gabirol is known to the intellectual world of Europe through his philosophical book *Fons vitae* (Source of Life). His name was corrupted to Avicebron, and it was not until the nineteenth century that Avicebron was identified as Ibn Gabirol. No one had dreamed that the author whose works had had so great an influence on medieval Christian theology, mainly by the transmission of Aristotelian and Neoplatonic thought, was a Jew.

The caliphate of Cordova came to an unhappy end in 1031 after a long period of anarchy. The region split up into a number of small kingdoms, the Taifas, which were constantly at war either against one another or against the Christian states in northern Spain. The *reconquista,* or struggle of the northern states to recapture the country from Islamic dominion, entered a critical phase when, in 1085, Alfonso VI of Castile conquered Toledo. To avert the danger the Taifas called upon the Almoravides, rulers of Morocco, for help.

The Christian advance was held up but not pushed back by the conquests of the Almoravides and their successors, the Almohades. But these North African fellow-Moslems soon became themselves oppressors; they suppressed the Taifas and by the end of the eleventh century their dominion extended over the whole Muslim region in the Peninsula.

The kingdom of the Almoravides collapsed barely sixty years after their arrival before the assault of the Almohades (1147). Both were Muslim Berber tribes and as such were possessed by a fanatical, ascetic and puritanical spirit that led them to insist inexorably on the conversion of all 'unbelievers' to Islam. Reaction followed the religious tolerance of the caliphate, and a large proportion of the Jews in the Islamic south migrated to the Christian states of the north, where they were recognized as citizens with equal rights by the enlightened and tolerant kings of Castile, Navarre and Aragon. Soon, as previously under the caliphate, they were occupying important posts in public service and commerce. The intelligent policy of toleration which Alfonso VI and his successors applied to the newly conquered Arab territories contributed materially to their rapid assimilation and integration; the Arabic-speaking Jewish refugees who were settled mainly in these areas were able to play a valuable part as mediators between the Arabs and their Christian rulers.

Amongst these refugees was the Rabbi Moses ben Maimon, known as Maimonides (1135–1204), the most famous Jewish philosopher of the Middle Ages. Unlike most of the others, he had taken refuge with his family in North Africa and finally, after long wandering, became court physician in Cairo to Sultan Saladin, the great opponent of the Crusaders.

Moses ben Maimon was an extremely systematic thinker. His *Mishneh Thora,* or second Torah, is a methodical compilation of the whole of traditional teaching. In his work *More ha Nebuchim* (Guide for the Perplexed), Maimonides evolved a philosophy of Judaism, an attempt at a synthesis between Aristotelian philosophy and the Jewish religion of the Law. The logical method he used significantly influenced medieval theology and philosophy, especially that of Thomas Aquinas.

Even during his lifetime Maimonides was the object of intense veneration by the Jews, as is proved by the saying, coined at that time, 'From Moses (the law-giver) to Moses there was no one like Moses'. But there were detractors enough. Jewish orthodoxy was sharply critical, declaring that to use philosophical-rational methods of thought was not compatible with the teaching revealed by God on Sinai. The Dominican Order, founded in 1216, banned the works of Maimonides as inimical to the faith and decreed that they should be burnt (1234).

In the spheres of geography and astronomy, too, there were important Jewish scholars. The best-known is Benjamin of Tudela. Between the years 1160 and 1173 he travelled in the Mediterranean countries and in the Near East and wrote an account of every Jewish community that he visited. His work is of great historical value in regard to the *diaspora*.

Amongst the large number of significant men who were active during this fertile epoch, both in Islamic and later in Christian Spain, mention must be made of Jehuda ha-Levi (*c.* 1075–1141), the greatest Hebrew poet of the Middle Ages. He was born in Toledo where, after the conquest of the city by Alfonso VI in 1085, he experienced that fruitful symbiosis between Orient and Occident which resulted from the rule of farseeing monarchs such as Alfonso VIII and Ferdinand III. The cultivated, open-minded atmosphere of Toledo, exceptional in the Middle Ages, inspired and fructified the genius of the poet. His hymns are dedicated to God, to the soul and to the people.

Maimonides (1135–1204), religious philosopher, man of learning and doctor. Born at Cordova, he escaped from the fanatical Almohades to North Africa and later became personal physician at the court of Sultan Saladin. Woodcut with Maimonides' signature.

NIGHT-TIME

As, little since, I wakeful lay and thought on thee,
Thy blessings in a round appeared to me;
And they—proclaim the miracle!—me clearly taught
Thine image, soul, are both in me enwrought.
And did my faithful heart not look on thee
As it had been on Sinai?
I sought thy countenance
Which in its brilliance,
Descended in a cloud to pass me by;
When, by my musing driven from my bed,
Before thy splendour, Lord, I bowed my head.

It is told of Jehuda ha-Levi that at an advanced age he abandoned family, wealth and a respected position in order to follow his yearning for Zion. After endless pains he reached the gates of Jerusalem when, on the point of entering the Holy City, he was transfixed by the spear of a charging Saracen horseman.

The humane and tolerant attitude of the Christian states in the eleventh and twelfth centuries was reversed when at the beginning of the thirteenth century the crusading spirit arrived in the country and the papal policy of oppression, ratified by the fourth Lateran Council in 1215, was taken up in Spain. An important part was played by the newly founded Dominican Order, which saw as its allotted task the fight against

… Know then that everything
takes place according to His pleasure,
notwithstanding that our acts
are in our power.
How so?
Just as it was the pleasure of the Creator
that fire and air shall ascend,
earth and water descend,
and that the spheres
shall revolve in a circle,
and all other things
in the Universe shall exist
in their special ways which He desired,
so it was His pleasure
that Man should have liberty
of will, and all his acts
should be left to his discretion;
that nothing should coerce him
or draw him to aught.

From *The Strong Hand* by Maimonides.

OLOMBVS LYCVR-NO ORBIS REPTO

'August 2nd was the day of the great Jewish exodus.... Hundreds of thousands left on that fateful date, some to rebuild their fortunes in other lands, others to suffer martyrdom at the hands of pirate or Saracen. And on that date, which saw the affliction of Israel, Colon also chose to embark. He left the Spanish soil for his high mission on the same day the Jews left it for their second exodus.'

From *Christopher Columbus* by Salvador de Madariaga. The question of Columbus' Jewish descent has been repeatedly the object of detailed investigations but has never been finally resolved. But in his book Madariaga, basing his conclusions on the most recent research, leaves no room for doubt that Columbus really was a Jew.

Christopher Columbus (after Sebastiano del Piombo).

Marranos ('Despised ones') was the name for Spanish Jews who adopted Christianity under threat of death, while secretly remaining true to the faith of their fathers. A murmured prayer or the wearing of festive clothes on the sabbath was enough to betray the heretic to the Inquisition. Under torture many confessed their faults; thousands, however, stood fast and died in the flames of the Auto-da-Fé.

Wood-engraving from the nineteenth century.

heretics and Jews. It was also the vehicle of the Inquisition after 1231, providing its jurists and administrators for several centuries.

One of its members was Vincente Ferrer, a fanatical predicant friar who traversed the country with a great band of flagellants, invading synagogues and offering communities the alternative of conversion or death. Thus in 1411 he brought the great community of Toledo to the verge of annihilation. During a service he forced his way into the synagogue Sta Maria la Blanca, followed by a mob and brandishing in one hand a cross and in the other a Torah scroll. Thousands who refused apostasy were murdered when they were hurled down the steep cliffs above the Tagus.

Many Jews simulated conversion to Christianity. These were the many *marranos* of whom the majority adhered to their former religious practices. Upon these the Inquisition, doubting the sincerity of their conversion, turned their special attention. Many refused, even under excruciating torture, to admit that they were renegades from the Christian faith, and were burned to death in the Auto-da-Fé (act of faith). Others languished in the dungeons.

When, however, the inquisitors' instruments of torture and the 'acts of faith' at the stake failed to bring about any significant christianization of Spanish Jewry, the all-powerful Grand Inquisitor of the Catholic monarchs Ferdinand and Isabella, the Dominican Torquemada, decided to expel the Jews from Spain. There is a tradition that at the last moment the tax farmer, Abraham Senior and the finance minister Isaac Abrabanel, two of the most influential Jews, tried to avert the disaster by offering Ferdinand and Isabella a fantastically large sum of money. As both were showing signs of agreement, Torquemada rushed into the audience chamber holding a crucifix above his head, enjoining them: 'Look upon the Lord. Judas sold him for thirty pieces of silver, and you wish to sell him for thirty thousand. Here he is, take him and barter him away!' Ferdinand and Isabella signed the edict of expulsion on 31 March 1492.

Jews were to leave the country within four months. They were allowed to take no valuables, neither gold nor silver, with them. They could only dissipate what they possessed. Taking nothing except the clothes they were wearing and the little that they could carry, they left.

It was especially in the countries of the Levant under Turkish overlordship that the Spanish Jews took refuge. New Jewish communities arose throughout the Turkish empire, as in Salonica, Constantinople and Bursa (Prusa), and existing communities were stirred into new life. Many of the refugees returned to the Holy Land for which during centuries they had nostalgically longed. It had been incorporated into the Turkish empire in 1516. Important communities grew up in the four 'holy cities' of the country, Jerusalem, Hebron, Tiberias and Safed. A minority fled to northern countries, England, Scandinavia, Holland, Germany and the south of France. Amsterdam became the most important of the communities. Even the *marranos,* although they were *conversos* or converts and no doors were closed to them, often preferred (clandestine) emigration to a hypocritical and disingenuous existence. Most of them returned to Judaism, sometimes after several decades.

In the sixteenth century the Turkish empire had risen to be the most powerful state in Europe. Under the Sultans' farseeing policy, everything was done to encourage immigration, and Jews found entry to almost all the professions, and soon the sought-after Jewish craftsmen and traders were joined by Jewish doctors, ambassadors and interpreters. For the first time Jews began to play an important, if not crucial, role in international politics.

One of the outstanding figures among the Sephardic Jews, as the Spanish and Portuguese emigrants were called, was Joseph ha-Nassi. Originally a *marrano,* he and his family had reached Constantinople from Portugal by way of Antwerp and Amsterdam. There he threw off all pretence of Catholicism and, together with the whole of his family, reverted to the Jewish faith. After a few years at the court of Suleiman the Magnificent, he rose to be one of the most influential figures in the Turkish empire. Wherever he was able, he made use of diplomatic intervention to protect his co-religionists of the European *diaspora* against oppression. He obtained from Suleiman the concession of Tiberias and an adjoining piece of territory as a place for Jewish settlement. He fortified the town, planted mulberry trees for the production of silk and attempted to build up a textile industry. Even though his plans were to end in failure, they represent the earliest example of systematic Jewish resettlement in the Holy Land and as such were the prototype for all future times.

Most of those who returned to Palestine saw their true and real purpose in life as the study of the Torah. Year after year the communities sent emissaries (*Schlichim*) into the *diaspora* who maintained contact between the Holy Land and Jewry throughout the whole world. Safed, high up in the mountains of Galilee, became the new religious centre. This was the seat of Jewish mysticism, the Kabbalah, which was studied and interpreted in the small prayer-chambers and the synagogues of Safed. Its greatest teacher was Isaac Luria, known as Ari (1534–72). He gathered around him a group of chosen disciples who revered him as a holy man. As he wrote nothing down himself, his sayings were handed down by word of mouth by his disciples, and some were recorded in writing.

One of his most enthusiastic pupils, himself an important religious figure, was Joseph Caro (1488–1575). His work is a systematic condensation of the Talmud called *Schulchan Aruch* (Set Table). Upon this the social and religious life of Jewry has been based ever since.

It is not surprising that times of distress should cause men to resort to mysticism. It represents a kind of flight from the world and was a deep consolation to the Jews in their affliction. Ever since the second century A.D. there had been commentaries on the Bible that took the form of secret, mystical speculations. But Judaism took too practical a view of life to permit mysticism to gain the upper hand. Now, however, in times of utmost stress, it acquired a great following. It is not surprising that this too was a time of false Messiahs who again revived the religious hopes of the Jews.

The best known of them is Sabbatai Zevi (1626–76), the son of a well-to-do merchant of Smyrna (Asia Minor). In his youth he had learnt Kabbalah and in 1648 at the age of twenty-one he proclaimed his mission. In spite of the fact that he had been excommunicated by the horrified rabbis of Smyrna, had been accused of blasphemy and banished from the country, he acquired hordes of devoted disciples throughout the world of the *diaspora*. Messianic expectation spread like wildfire through the ghettos of Europe and the oriental communities. The mass of the people, the poorest of the poor, invested their last hope in the saviour.

In 1665, Sabbatai Zevi declared that the following year he would depose the sultan and lead the Jews back to Zion. And indeed the next year he actually went to Constantinople where the Turkish authorities at once put him in chains and threw him into prison. Faced with the alternative between death and apostasy to Islam, he chose the latter, to the bitter disappointment of his vast following. But many saw in Sabbatai Zevi's new faith only the will of God and themselves went over to Islam. This sect, called Donmeh, has survived up till today in Turkey. They played an active part in the Young Turk movement.

The term *Kabbalah* embraces the mystical teaching of Jewry, together with its movement and literature, which had evolved since late antiquity. Especially after the twelfth century, its doctrines were set down in many books, the most significant being the 'Zohar' (Splendour) which, beside the Bible and the Talmud, is the most important book in religious literature. It is presumed to have been compiled by the Spanish mystic, Moses de Leon, in the thirteenth century from ancient sources and contains essentially mystical annotations on the Pentateuch, the Song of Solomon, the Book of Ruth and Lamentations.

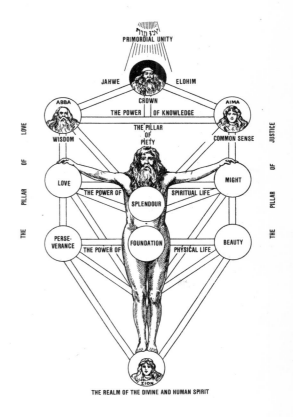

THE REALM OF THE DIVINE AND HUMAN SPIRIT

Kabbalistic teaching is esoteric speculation concerned on the one hand with divine matters and their poetical-mystical interpretation, and on the other with a philosophical-mystical interpretation of the creation. This is seen in the form of a 'Sephiroth tree', a kind of tree of life, symbolizing the archetype of the material world and of earthly man, Adam Kadmon (Primordial Man). The ten 'Sephiroth' (numbers) represent the stages of existence. The Sephiroth tree thus becomes the symbol of organic unity between physical and metaphysical being, so that, however much speculation it may contain, the Kabbalah never loses sight of the original Jewish concept of the unity of all things.

In the sixteenth century, Safed in Galilee became the centre of the Kabbalistic movement. Its most important exponent was Isaac Luria, known as Ari. Its insistence on the need to prepare for the kingdom of God by prayer and fulfilment of the Law led to the Messianic movements of the seventeenth century, which were to bring about the profoundest disruption within Jewry.

HATED, PERSECUTED, REVILED, AND OPPRESSED

The *Sachsenspiegel*, Germany's most important book of law in the Middle Ages (c. 1225), was compiled by Eike von Repgow. It maintained, in contrast to the Early Fathers who held the generally accepted view of 'Jewish servitude' (Servitus Judaeorum), that Jews were in fact the equal of other men, for since all are created in the likeness of God, all must be equal.

Where judgment is not governed by royal decree, any man of blameless reputation may be judge; only the Wend and the Saxon have no jurisdiction over each other. (*Landrecht* III, 70, 1)

Above, a Jew (tall hat and beard), a Frank (fur collar), and a Saxon (with knife) appear before the earl while a Wend (wearing leg-bands) stands apart.

CAPTIONS TO COLOUR PLATES

Page 117: Acre, arched entrance to the Khan el Afranj (French caravanserai) from the time of the Crusades (twelfth–thirteenth century).

Page 118: Vault in the Romanesque church at Abu Ghosh near Jerusalem (time of the Crusades, first half of the twelfth century).

Page 119: Crusaders' ceramics: fragment of a glazed bowl of the twelfth century with a primitive design of a head (Acre Museum); glazed bowl from Cyprus (twelfth century) with ornamented cross (Haaretz Museum, Tel Aviv); glazed bowl from Cyprus (twelfth century) with picture of nobleman (?) (Haaretz Museum); fragment of a glazed bowl of the thirteenth century (Acre Museum).

Page 120: Acre. Refectory of the Order of St. John — 'Crypt of St. John' (mid-twelfth century).

In the early Middle Ages, Jews were agents of trade between east and west. This important economic function afforded them a relative amount of security both in the countries of Islam and in the empire of Charlemagne and the countries which succeeded it. Yet in some places they were fiercely persecuted.

With the increasing power of the papacy during the twelfth and thirteenth centuries, the Jew's social position changed fundamentally. The third Lateran Council of 1179 and the fourth of 1215 laid the foundations for the future anti-Jewish policy of the Church.

The third Lateran Council's first preoccupation was to combat the heretical Albigensian movement which had taken hold in the south of France and was menacing the Church of Rome. Jews were accused of being in league with the Albigensians, and this was seen as a justification for the revival of the old restrictive and discriminatory laws of Byzantine times which, in the course of seven hundred years, had fallen more or less into desuetude. No Jew was allowed to take service with a Christian or to employ a Christian. Further, Christians were forbidden to live among Jews and the way was thus prepared for the later ghetto system. In addition, the fourth Lateran Council excluded Jews from any public office which might have lent them some kind of authority.

In order to complete the isolation of the Jews within the Christian world, the Council laid down that they should wear a red or yellow badge. In Italy, Germany and Austria, Jews were also compelled to wear a tall, cylindrical hat of a definite colour.

The Dominican Order, which we have already had occasion to mention, must again be indicated as an instrument of Jewish oppression and persecution. It had been set up to combat heretical movements, but after the suppression of the Albigensians in 1229 it concentrated its attentions on Jewry. It staged public discussions on religious questions between its own representatives and Jews, of which the outcome was prearranged, and the participating Jews only endangered their persons. Dominican monks forced their way into synagogues and preached sermons on conversion, to which the congregation was compelled to listen. The Order censored Jewish religious writing and in Paris on 17 June 1242, before the whole court, twenty-four waggon loads of priceless manuscripts of the Talmud and other religious works were publicly burnt at the instigation of the Dominicans. It was a mortal blow from which the cultural life of medieval Jewry never recovered. Only one complete medieval manuscript of the Talmud has survived till our times.

Under the medieval feudal system and the urban rule of the guilds, Jews were completely without rights. Excluded from all Christian callings that were subject to the guilds, there was nothing they could do but turn to the activity of money lending, proscribed by the Church ever since the third Lateran Council, which, by forbidding interest charges, had made this profession untenable by Christians.

Having no rights and standing outside society, they were at the ruler's mercy. They were bondsmen to the king *(servi camerae regis)* and he could do with them what he wanted. They became a source of revenue from which the coffers of state could be replenished as soon as they were empty and the extravagance of the court made good. At the same time, being 'usurers' as all money-lenders were described, Jews aroused the hatred and envy of the people, for as givers of credit they had become indispensable to both secular and ecclesiastical circles. Kings and princes tolerated and protected Jews so long as they continued to serve and to provide. When they had been sucked dry they had to be got rid of. Medieval history is full of accounts of their expulsions.

In England Edward I expelled the then quite destitute Jews in 1290. None were permitted to return until 1656, in the time of Oliver Cromwell. This alternation during the course of centuries of expulsion and readmission is found in its most grotesque form in France. In 1182 Philip II Augustus drove the Jews out of his domain which then comprised only the Ile-de-France. In 1198, on his return from the Third Crusade, he recalled them to help put his disrupted finances in order again. Charles VI, by a decree of 17 September 1394, finally drove them out of France after the Jews of Paris had been accused of persuading one of their number, an apostate to Christianity, to revert to his own faith.

Until the revolution of 1789 there were few Jews in the French provinces. Only after that date were they granted the right to settle.

In Germany, which was split up into a great many small states with a resulting lack of political unity, there could be no question of general expulsion as in England and France. But it often happened that one or other of the electors, dukes or bishops would drive the Jews out of his territory, when they would take refuge in a neighbouring state, only to be driven thence soon after. From a historical point of view, however, Germany presents a typical picture of Jewish martyrdom.

Widespread Jewish persecution had already begun with the Crusades. The first victims were the flourishing communities on the Rhine: Mainz, Worms, Cologne, Speyer and the communities of Champagne in northern France.

The succession of Jewish massacres was now almost continuous, reaching a tragic climax in 1348, the year of the Black Death. Jews were accused of poisoning wells. In Chillon in the south of France a Jew admitted under torture that the poison was made up of frogs, squirrels, spiders, human flesh, the hearts of Christians and consecrated bread, and had been distributed among Jewish communities. The insane accusation spread like wildfire throughout the empire, with the most ghastly consequences. One hundred and fifty small communities and sixty large ones were wiped out. A few succeeded in escaping to Poland. In Basle the whole community was herded into a wooden barn on one of the islands in the Rhine and burnt alive, while the Strasbourg community was consumed in a holocaust in the Jewish cemetery. So as not to fall into the hands of their persecutors, the Jews of Worms set fire to their houses and killed themselves. The same thing happened in 1349 in Cologne.

Pope Clement VI tried in vain to stem the madness by promulgating a Bull.

Every natural catastrophe, plague or famine, every war, every unexplained crime, was laid at their door, and they were also accused of being in league with heretics. Ritual murder and desecration of the Host were almost standing accusations. Although the popes repeatedly denounced both as slanderous lies, they have continued to persist until the present day, and thousands have fallen victim to this primitive delusion, the offspring of an archaic mixture of magic and religious ideas. Jews

The outer form of the Talmud faithfully reflects its process of growth throughout the centuries. At the centre of each page is the text of the Mishnah, to the right of this the interpretation of the Gemara; Rashi's (1040–1105) commentary, which was added to all editions of the Talmud about a century after his death, appears to the left of the centre column. The outer margins to the left and below contain the Tosafoth ('Additions'), that is to say, the commentaries of many schools of learning between the twelfth and fourteenth centuries.

The Munich Talmud of 1343 is the only complete edition surviving from the Middle Ages; all the others were seized and burnt on the orders of the temporal and ecclesiastical authorities.

The first printed edition of the Talmud, edited between 1520 and 1523 by Daniel Bomberg in Venice, appeared with the express permission of Pope Leo X. Not long afterwards, one of his successors put a ban on this edition and all previous copies of the Talmud.

charged with ritual murder were supposed to drink the blood of a Christian boy while performing certain magic rituals, and mixing it with unleavened bread at the Feast of the Passover.

The desecration of the Host was a crime born of the doctrine laid down by the fourth Lateran Council to the effect that the consecrated Host represented the body of Christ. It was now alleged that Jews stole the Host and abused it, in a repetition of Christ's death on the cross. Traces of red—mould formations on the bread—were described as blood-stains and were regarded as proof of abuse by Jews.

Only in Italy were Jews able to live in comparative safety, and more especially within the Papal States which were governed directly by the pope.

Although the policy of the Church was hostile towards the Jews, popes repeatedly called for mercy and moderation, and it was in effect only the Counter-reformation popes who revealed a disposition that was markedly anti-Jewish.

The tragedy of medieval Jewry culminated, as has already been mentioned, in the expulsion of Spanish Jews in 1492 by the Catholic monarchs Ferdinand and Isabella.

It must be supposed that in many places, normal human intercourse continued in everyday life between Jew and Christian whatever the hatred and enmity, the massacres and expulsions. The existence of a Jewish *minnesinger,* Süsskind of Trimberg, who was welcomed even at the courts of the aristocracy, throws a more kindly light on the picture, so harsh in other respects, of medieval Jewry.

Jewish populations occupied their own quarters of the towns. This was partly the result of the Church's segregation policy, but it also corresponded to the natural requirements of a group having all its interests, whether of a religious or secular character, in common.

In Spain, as well as in Cracow in Poland, there were enclosed Jewish quarters but it was only from the sixteenth century onwards that Jews began to be shut up in ghettos. In 1516, Jews in Venice were allotted as their quarter part of the town known as the Ghetto Nuovo (new foundry). The term ghetto became commonly used to describe enclosed Jewish quarters in the towns. The ghetto system spread rapidly in Italy and the rest of Europe, especially after Pope Pius IV had issued a Bull in 1555, at the time of the Counter-reformation, which restored all previous restrictions and added some new ones.

The gates were closed after sunset and no Jew was allowed to remain outside the ghetto walls.

As the size of the ghettos could not be increased, they were apt to become uncomfortably overcrowded and taller houses had to be built.

Life in the ghetto reflected every aspect of the outside world. School attendance was generally enforced. There were troupes of players and choirs both within and outside the synagogue. But religious life was paramount, with regular visits to the synagogue, festivals and daily lessons.

Baruch Spinoza (1632–1677), with Maimonides, is the greatest philosopher of Jewish extraction. His forbears were Portuguese *marranos* who emigrated to Amsterdam; he himself was excommunicated from the Jewish community in 1656 for 'terrible heresies'.
Anonymous painting.

Spinoza's philosophy is based on a unified view of the world: God is the only, eternal, infinite substance, and God and Nature are identical *(Deus sive natura);* this concept of unity probably derived from the Judaistic idea of unity. God, however, is seen as an abstraction, not as a being; in Spinoza's principal work, the *Ethics,* this is deduced in a system of definition, principle, proposition and proof.

The view of Spinoza as a cool, detached philosopher is not borne out by his doctrine of active and passive affects (emotions). This thinker, with his deep knowledge of humankind, saw the power of the active affect, which overcomes the destructive passive affect, as man's capacity to use his intellect to know God, who loves himself in us *(amor intellectualis Dei).*

This herding together of all social classes without regard to education or fortune was bound to lead eventually to social and intellectual narrowness and to a form of physical and mental inbreeding that was intolerable. Poets and thinkers who had outgrown the narrow confines of the ghetto and had made contact with the intellectual world of Europe, men like Baruch Spinoza and Uriel Acosta in Amsterdam, stood outside the community. Both paid for the new-won intellectual freedom with excommunication.

Liberation from the ghetto was first brought about by the French Revolution in 1789 and the dawn of emancipation.

POLISH JEWRY

Excavations on the Crimean peninsula disclosed gravestones with Hebrew inscriptions and symbols such as the seven-branched candelabrum, showing that as early as Roman-Hellenistic times Jews had settled in south Russia. The Jewish communities of the peninsula flourished considerably because of their position as agents of Byzantine-Russian trade.

To the east of them, between the Black Sea and the Caspian, lived the people of the Khazars. When in the eighth century they followed the example of their monarch Bulan and adopted the Jewish faith, the Jewish population of south Russia grew appreciably. But between A.D. 965 and 969 the campaigns of the prince of Kiev brought the Khazar kingdom to a violent end. The Khazars survived for another hundred years in the Crimean peninsula where they had taken refuge, but were eventually driven out, during a short-lived Russo-Byzantine alliance, by the combined forces of the latter.

The extent of the impact made by the distant Jewish kingdom of the Khazars is evident from the correspondence of Hasdai ibn Shaprut, Physician of Abd-er-Rahman III in Cordova with the then king of the Khazars, Joseph. And in the twelfth century Jehuda ha-Levi in his book *Al-Chazari* recalls the conversion of King Bulan.

Mieszko III, Duke of Gnesen (1173–1202), after acquiring the overlordship of Poland, imposed a currency reform of a revolutionary nature which so upset the people that war broke out and Mieszko himself had to flee the country. In 1181 he won Gnesen back with the help of Pomerania.

His campaign must have had the financial support of the Jews, since for twenty years subsequently they were responsible for the ducal mint. They took advantage of this to mint their own bracteates, coins stamped on one side only, and bearing Hebrew inscriptions, which are unique in the history of Christian Europe. The coin shown above has the head of Mieszko with a lion and the Hebrew inscription 'Mieszko, King of Poland'.

Little is known of the history of the Jews in Russia and Poland during the next two centuries. There is evidence of the movement of Jewish communities northwards as far as Poland and Lithuania, and there is mention of a flourishing Jewish community in Gnesen, then capital of Poland. There were Jewish tax farmers and coin makers, and in the twelfth century there was even Polish coinage with Hebrew inscriptions.

In the course of the following centuries, wave upon wave of refugees arrived in the Jewish communities of Poland from the west; in the twelfth and thirteenth they were fleeing before the massacres of the Crusaders, and after 1348 from the persecutions arising from the plague.

Jews from the west spoke a kind of Middle High German enriched with Hebrew and Slav words. This language became general throughout the Polish and east Jewish communities and has survived until today under the designation of Yiddish.

Poland's economy had suffered enormously under the attacks of the Mongols and the Polish kings were glad of the Jews' financial expertise both in a practical and advisory capacity. Jews were employed as land-agents by the high aristocracy, and as administrators of salt and other types of mine; they were tax farmers and moneylenders, and as agents in distant countries they organized the sale of surplus agricultural products such as grain, cotton, timber for building and furs.

Sample of the Yiddish language common to east European Jewish communities:

… Mein seln zu got an der wartung zu dem morgen, di do warten zu dem morgen. Es hoft Jisroel zu got wen mit im ist di gnad und viel mit im der losung. Und er sol losen Jisroel von alen seinen sunden.

(My soul is in God in expectation of the morning, with those who await the morning. Israel's hope is in God with whom is mercy and manifold salvation. And He shall deliver Israel from all her sins.)

(PSALM 31, in the Yiddish translation of the *Codex de Rossi*, 1513, in the Regia Biblioteca at Parma.)

The Cossack commander Bogdan Chmielnicki (1648–51) led a revolt of the Ukraine
against Polish oppression in 1648/9; this was
accompanied by terrible massacres of the Jewish population.

Anonymous painting.

They were under the protection of a royal patent issued by Boleslaus the Pious in
1264. This patent was confirmed and its terms expanded by Casimir the Great
(1333–70). Jews had complete freedom of movement and their commerce was quite
unrestricted. Their physical existence and possessions were under the especial protection of the king. The desecration of synagogues and cemeteries was specifically forbidden, and the charge of ritual murder was denounced as a slanderous falsehood.

Thus the Jews enjoyed a large measure of autonomy. In 1551, Sigismund Augustus
allowed them to choose their own Chief Rabbi and their own judges. In this way the
Jewish communities obtained self-government including a judiciary that accorded
with rabbinical law. After this even state taxes were collected by the communities
themselves.

The great Lublin and Yaroslav markets, where crowds of Jews gathered, made
suitable occasions for the sitting of the *Vaad*, a supreme council of thirty-eight members
(fourteen rabbis and twenty-four laymen). This saw to the overall organization of the
communities. It arbitrated in disputes within or between individual communities and
shared out the burden of taxation between them.

This council became a kind of parliament for Polish Jewry, and its authority in
the moral and religious affairs of the communities was undisputed. Educational matters were in its hands and it controlled the printing of Hebrew books, the import of
books from abroad and protected copyright.

As always when Jewry was able to develop with reasonable freedom, cultural life
flourished. There was no community, however small, without its own *cheder* (teaching
room) or its own *Yeshivah* (religious academy), where Torah and Talmud were
devotedly studied and discussed. Each community was responsible for looking after
the young scholars. They were invited by every family in turn to daily meals and on
feast-days, or they found board and lodging in a benevolent institution. Every adult
scholar was under an obligation to instruct at least two boys so as to gain practice
in the interpretation and explication of the Torah. They were also in constant touch
with the director of the Yeshivah and its individual teachers. They learnt for learning's sake and an educated rabbi was not a paid official; he received no kind of salary.

From this popularization and democratization of spiritual teaching, which reached
a degree never before attained and was peculiar to Polish Jewry, a special method of
teaching arose which was known as *pilpul*, an extreme form of dialectic. Discussions
were held for the sake of argument rather than for the sake of knowledge, so that the
method was apt to lead to the absurd. But it enabled individuals to develop great
intellectual attainments and helped to make their minds acute and agile.

This picture of Polish Jewry had its darker side—the hostile opposition of the
Church, of the urban middle classes and of the lesser aristocracy. The Church endeavoured to impose its usual anti-Jewish policy and the burgesses, amongst them many
German merchants, and the lesser aristocracy, regarded the success of Jewish traders
with a jealous eye.

The enmity of the major section of the population sometimes broke out in the form
of accusations of ritual murder and on occasion there were massacres. In 1407 the
Jewish community of Cracow was wiped out. The only survivors were those who
consented to be baptized.

With the decline of the Polish kingdom the position of the Jews deteriorated
steadily. Their free trade was restricted, they were excluded from public office and
many towns expelled them altogether.

This century-long relative flowering of Polish Jewry came to a tragic end between
1648 and 1651 with the pogroms of the *hetman* Bogdan Chmielnicki and his Cossacks.
Their cynicism and cruelty exceeded anything that had been experienced before.

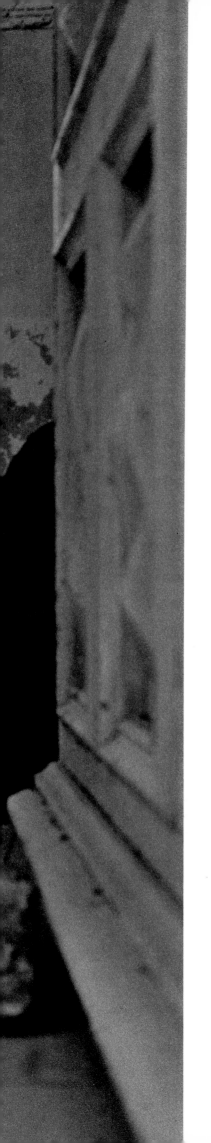

Starting as a revolt of the Ukrainian Cossacks against their feudal oppressors, it became increasingly a pogrom against the Jews who were alleged to be in league with the nobility. It is believed that about half the Jewish population of Ukraine and Galicia—some two hundred to four hundred thousand souls—were slaughtered.

A few years later, in 1655—following the Swedish invasion of White Russia and Lithuania—Polish patriots fell upon what remained of the Jews who were accused of making common cause with the Swedes. In many towns the Jewish inhabitants were either exterminated or expelled. 'For it is written: Yea, for thy sake are we killed all the day long; we are counted as sheep for the slaughter' (Psalm 44, 22), wrote rabbi Samuel Auerbach, who survived the Lublin bloodbath.

In the second half of the eighteenth century there was another revolt of Ukrainian peasants under Cossack leadership against their aristocratic oppressors. This was the rising of the Haidamaks, and once again their hatred vented itself on the Jews.

In this time of persecution and of cultural and economic decline, Polish Jewry found strength for a spiritual revival in Hasidism (piety). Inspired by Jewish mysticism (Kabbalah) which had evolved two centuries before in Safed, the movement was chiefly a reaction against the purely rational study of the Talmud.

Its founder was Israel ben Eliezer, called Baal Shem Tov, who lived about 1700–60. His life is so surrounded by legend that today it is difficult to distinguish history from myth. His great achievement was to bring back the mass of the people from their one-sided intellectual preoccupation with the Torah and to lead them back to the original sources of the faith.

Of simple origin and without any thorough knowledge of the Talmud, his was a charismatic personality of unusual power. He performed miracles and healed the sick. People came to him in their hundreds and he was venerated as a holy man. His teaching has a strong pantheistic streak. He was deeply involved with nature and in all things, even in the least of them, he saw God's creation which should be joyously worshipped.

He held that what is evil in life is not truly evil, but is the lowest rung on the ladder of the good, and sin only arises out of ignorance: that piety does not consist in literal obedience to the letter of the Law, but in the measure of each individual's spiritual and emotional participation which, attaining ecstasy, can be expressed in the dance.

Israel ben Eliezer had no desire at all to create a religious movement. He gathered about him a circle of pupils who recorded his teachings and his sayings and it was they who were the actual founders of the movement.

His successors were the *Zaddikim* or righteous who, as leaders of the group, surrounded themselves with a veritable household and made their office hereditary. Thus the Zaddikim dynasties grew up, some of whom still exist in America and in Israel.

The rabbinic Jewry of Poland strongly opposed Hasidism. But an eventual *rapprochement* was inevitable. Traditional Jewish religion, threatened with rigidity and mere formalism, experienced a revival, while out of the ranks of Hasidism came exceptionally able scholars who were in all ways equal to the rabbis in the teaching of the Talmud.

The religious Hasidic movement was a popular movement which upheld the right of the simple, uneducated man to his personal religion. It was a revolution from below, and it saved Judaism from sclerosis and stagnation.

Israel ben Eliezer, known as Baal Shem Tov (Master of the Divine Name), lived in Podolia (1700–60). His charismatic personality made him the centre and inspiration of a circle of disciples, the founders of Hasidism.
Contemporary, anonymous portrait.

Why do we say 'Our God and God of our fathers?' There are two kinds of men who believe in God. One believes because of the tradition handed down to him by his fathers, and his belief is strong. The other comes to belief by inquiry. And the difference between them is this: the advantage of the first is that his belief cannot be shaken, whatever argument may be brought against it, for his belief is firm, having come to him from his fathers; but it has one imperfection, namely that his belief is but a human injunction, and has been learnt without sense or understanding. The advantage of the second is that, having found God by his own intense seeking, he has achieved belief by himself; but here too lies an imperfection: it is a simple matter to shake his belief by contrary proof. But he who unites both, is unassailable. This is why we say: 'Our God', meaning our seeking, and 'God of our fathers' meaning our tradition.

A saying of Baal Shem Tov, free rendering by Martin Buber.

IN RUSSIA

Murder of Tsar Alexander II. Contemporary wood engraving.

Alexander II's reign (1855–81) began, like that of Alexander I (1801–25), with a liberal policy. But whereas Alexander I did in fact issue a decree which for a time gave Jews the right to choose any profession they liked, allowed them entry to schools and universities, and gave them the right to own land and to build factories, the 'great reforms' announced by Alexander II and welcomed with such hopeful enthusiasm by Jews soon proved illusory. For their chief beneficiary was the Russian serf who, still remaining landless, competed with the marginal retail business of the Jew, now destitute as a result of Nicholas I's cruel régime. When Alexander II was assassinated in March 1881, a Jewish girl being among the accused, murderous pogroms ensued. As a result of these and of the 'May Laws' of 1882, Jews had no choice but to leave Russia.

Unlike Poland, Russia was never prepared to concede to Jews any right of settlement in her territory. Both people and rulers were imbued with superstitious prejudice against the Jewish people. In 1526, the Russian ambassador in Rome declared: 'The Muscovite people fears none so much as it fears the Jews and will not let them enter their country.'

With the partition of Poland between Austria, Prussia and Russia at the end of the eighteenth century, the major part of the Jewish population of Poland—perhaps nine hundred thousand people—became subject to Russian supremacy.

The Jewish policy of Tsarist Russia allied to the Russian orthodox Church meant the suppression of all the civic rights which to some degree had been enjoyed by Jews under Polish rule. The functions of the Jewish autonomous administration (*Kahal*) were restricted virtually to the extent of its acting merely as agent for the application of anti-Jewish measures.

It is true that the Tsars Paul I (1796–1801) and Alexander I (1801–25), under the influence of the European Enlightenment, endeavoured to implement a relatively more liberal policy, having as its object Jewish apostasy and amalgamation with the rest of the population. When this failed, however, Alexander I revoked all his liberal decrees such as the admission of Jews to agriculture and the crafts, and there began the dark age of Tsarist-orthodox reaction during the nineteenth and twentieth centuries.

Alexander's successor, Nicholas I (1825–55) attempted to solve the Jewish problem by the imposition of military service on the Jews. But instead of the usual twenty-five years they were forced to serve for thirty-one, and were conscripted at the age of twelve, or even eight, instead of the usual eighteen. What neither the government nor the Church had succeeded in doing, that is, to bring the Jews to apostasy, it was hoped the army sergeant would do. It was the task of the Kahal to conscript these children, tearing them from the arms of their parents. This barbaric decree was eventually abolished by the successor of Nicholas I, Alexander II (1855–81).

Jews were permitted to live only in a prescribed area, the Pale of Settlement, extending from the Crimea to the Baltic. A certain number of well-to-do Jews were given permission to settle in the interior of Russia, in Moscow or St. Petersburg, whence they were later to be expelled.

In 1882 the enactment of the scandalous May Laws struck a disastrous blow at Russian Jewry. A complete *numerus clausus* was imposed in regard to students at universities and pupils at higher schools, and new settlements in villages and rural areas were forbidden. The latter prohibition functioned in such a manner that any Jewish citizen returning from a journey was regarded as a 'new settler' and was refused entry. In consequence, these wretched men and their families were forced to go and live in the towns of the Pale where the mass of the Jewish proletariat became enormously swollen.

When Alexander II, who had mitigated or abolished some of the harsher anti-

Jewish measures, was assassinated by a Russian revolutionary in 1881, there began a period of pogroms that lasted until the October Revolution and the fall of the Tsar in 1917. The Union of the Russian People developed by prime minister Stolypin, whose instrument were bands of terrorists called 'the Black Hundred' by the people, made it their business to maintain a constant series of acts of violence and pogroms in areas of Jewish settlement.

In 1911 another ritual murder case was staged. It was brought against Mendel Beilis in Kiev. Not even a Russian court, however, was able to bring a verdict of guilty in face of overwhelming evidence to the contrary, and the accused was acquitted, but Jewry as such was naturally held responsible for the murder.

In face of the perpetual threat to life and property no choice remained but to flee. Between 1881 and 1914 an almost continuous stream of refugees flowed into the west. Before the turn of the century, nearly a million Jews had abandoned their former homes in eastern Europe.

They took refuge in the capitals of Europe, but their main objective was the Anglo-Saxon countries, England, America and Canada, where modern anti-Semitism had not yet taken root. Large Jewish quarters became established in both London and New York where for more than a generation Jews went on living in their old traditional way, speaking Yiddish as their principal language.

This colossal process of resettlement was rendered possible by the selfless devotion of Jewish aid organizations which provided the refugees with food and clothing and smoothed their way back to normal human existence. In England there was the Board of Deputies of British Jews and the Anglo-Jewish Organization, in France the *Alliance Israélite Universelle,* in Germany the *Hilfsverein der deutschen Juden,* and in America the American Jewish Joint Distribution Committee; what they achieved is beyond praise.

The 1914–18 war, the Russian Revolution and the fall of the Tsarist régime brought about fundamental changes for Russian Jewry.

The main theatres of war were along the Polish border and in the Pale of Settlement. Many Jewish communities were uprooted and forcibly deported by the Russians.

With the revolution in 1917 and the consequent resistance of 'White Russians' under generals Petlyura and Denikin there were widespread pogroms.

Half the Jewish population had become part of the new republic of Poland after the war. In both Russia and Poland they were now accorded equal rights, but this in practice, proved exceedingly difficult to implement. The vast majority of Jews, were small retailers for whom there was little place in the new Russia of workers and peasants.

Again, the religious loyalties of Russian Jewry were completely at variance with the ideas of the communist revolution. Even membership of the Zionist Movement was regarded as a crime against the revolution and was severely punished.

Attempts to settle urban populations on the land, and the plan to set up an autonomous Jewish republic in Birobidzhan in eastern Siberia failed from lack of support among the Jewish masses.

Robbed of its religious institutions, completely cut off from the rest of the world and restricted to urban occupations, Russian Jewry underwent a process of total assimilation and was no longer of any significance to world Jewry. Unlike other peoples in the Soviet Union, it did not have the good fortune to be recognized as a national minority. Yet the majority of the people have maintained contact with their own historic past, and the question of their national, social and religious future remains problematical.

Marc Chagall, the Russian-Jewish painter and graphic artist, was born in 1887 at Liosno near Vitebsk, of a poor and large family. The theme that underlies his art is the world of his childhood, the world of Hasidism and the Russian fairy-tale, which he transforms into visions of glowing colour. Chagall's bold inspiration made a decisive impact on Surrealism.

'Jew in Black and White', oil on canvas (1914).

Since Tsarist Russia held out little prospect of study or work for scientifically gifted young Jews, many Russian-Jewish scientists of world repute are numbered among the intellectual emigrants. Some of the most important were the mathematician Georg Cantor, to whose theory of quantity the English mathematical philosopher, Bertrand Russell, has acknowledged his indebtedness; the microbiologist Ilya Metchnikoff, who shared the Nobel Prize for medicine with Paul Ehrlich in 1908; Waldemar M. Haffkine, collaborator of Pascal, Ehrlich and Metchnikoff in Paris—his anti-cholera serum saved thousands of lives during the 1893 cholera epidemic in India.

It was easier for Jewish artists to make their way in Russia: thus the composer Henri Wieniawski was a teacher at the Petersburg Conservatory and his brother Joseph, also famous as a violinist, worked at the Moscow Institute. Jewish *virtuosi* of the violin such as Mischa Elman, Jascha Heifetz and many others are either of Russian origin or, like David Oistrakh, still live in Russia.

Of the vast number of Yiddish writers in Russia, we need only mention Shalom Aleichem, Sholem Asch and Sholem J. Abramovich (Mendele the Bookseller), the 'grandfather' of Yiddish literature.

Moses Mendelssohn (1729–86) left Dessau for Berlin at the age of fourteen. From 1754 he was a friend of Lessing's. In 1764 he won the Berlin Akademie der Wissenschaften award for his *Treatise on Evidence in the Metaphysical Sciences*, one of the other two unsuccessful contestants for the award being Immanuel Kant. Mendelssohn's writings initiated Jewish emancipation in Germany.

Contemporary wood engraving.

There is not, amongst all the precepts and tenets of the Mosaic laws, a single one which says, 'Thou shalt believe this', or 'Thou shalt not believe it', but they all say, 'Thou shalt do', or 'Thou shalt forbear'... All the commandments of the Mosaic Law are addressed to the will of man, and to his acting faculty.

From *Jerusalem: a Treatise on Religions Authority & Judaism* by Moses Mendelssohn.

CAPTIONS TO COLOUR PLATES

The seventeenth and eighteenth centuries are centuries of gradual transition, leading to the final emancipation of the Jewish people during the nineteenth and twentieth centuries. In this process an important part was played by the communities of *marranos* who had fled from the clutches of the Inquisition in Spain and Portugal, largely to settle in the major sea ports on the Atlantic and the North Sea, Bayonne, Bordeaux, Amsterdam, Hamburg and London.

As Catholics all careers were open to them and they quickly attained high positions in commerce, politics and science. Whole *marrano* communities returned to Judaism. In this manner they went a long way towards effacing the distinctions between Jew and Gentile, since they succeeded in maintaining equality of civic rights.

Another phenomenon of the transition was the so called *Hofjudentum* ('court Jewry'). At the end of the Thirty Years War in 1648, Germany had split up into a large number of principalities, some small, some tiny. These competed with each other in their endeavour to ape the court of Versailles. It became clear that the right people to put their state treasuries in order were Jews with a flair for finance. The few chosen for this purpose were accorded special privileges and were virtually on an equal footing with their Christian fellow-citizens, but the fortunes they acquired could not be inherited and fell to the Prince when they died.

Their fall, however, could be as sudden as their rise had been meteoric. The most notorious case is that of Joseph Oppenheimer, known as 'Jew Süss' (1698–1738). He was the factor of Duke Charles Alexander I of Württemberg. On the sudden death of his patron, he was arrested and sent to the gallows.

The rationalism and enlightenment of the eighteenth century did not fail also to attract Jews, the most important of these being Moses Mendelssohn (1729–86). He aimed at a *rapprochement* between Judaism and Christianity, and his principal work was the translation into German of the Pentateuch and the Psalms. These were written in Hebrew characters and their purpose was to teach his co-religionists High German, for Yiddish still remained their idiom. The commentary, however, was in Hebrew. Although he himself was a religious Jew conscious of tradition, he unwittingly brought about apostasy from Judaism. It is a significant fact that his own children and his grandson, Felix Mendelssohn-Bartholdy, the famous composer, went over to Christianity.

The decisive political event which finally demolished the ancient walls around the ghetto was the French Revolution of 1789. Although the declaration of human rights 'Liberty, Equality, Fraternity', was applicable to all classes, professions and religions without distinction, the principles could not be automatically put into effect; they had to be fought for. The Comte de Mirabeau, the Abbé Grégoire and the Comte de Clermont-Tonnerre fought tirelessly in the cause of equal rights for Jews. On 27 September 1791, after prolonged debates, the National Assembly accorded equal civic status to all Jews in the French Republic.

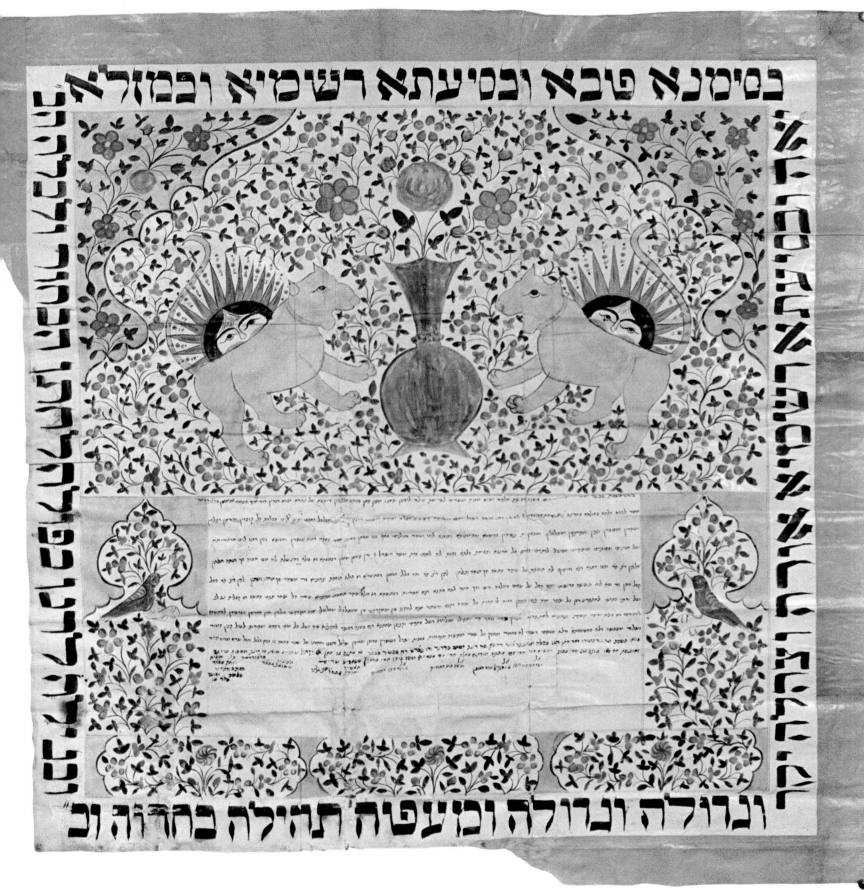

It was Napoleon who, through his campaigns and the foundation of new states, lent the force of law to the proclamation of equal rights for Jews in Europe. But the liberation of the Jews was regarded with suspicion and hostility by the people, and in Rome there were riots and protests.

With the collapse of the Napoleonic régime, Jews lost their equality of rights everywhere in Europe with the exception of the Netherlands which remained under French rule till 1814. The struggle for rights had to begin all over again. The wheel of history could not be turned back, however. Of greater significance than political events was the spirit of the times which bore the stamp of men like Voltaire, Rousseau, Lessing and Mendelssohn.

However immense the difficulties to be overcome, Jewish emancipation in the enlightened and liberal Europe of the nineteenth and twentieth centuries could no longer be retarded. In 1847 Jews in Prussia were recognized as citizens with equal rights on a basis of law, and Austria and Hungary followed suit in 1867. After 1871 the united German empire acknowledged the same principle. 1870 marked the final liberation of Jews in Italy. After a prolonged struggle the equality of rights for Jews at last received recognition in England in 1871. Switzerland followed in 1874.

America was the stronghold of modern liberal thought. After her discovery by Columbus in 1492 (the year when Spanish Jews were expelled), many *marranos* took refuge there. Most of them later returned to the Jewish faith. In 1654 the first group of Jews arrived in New Amsterdam, later New York. They formed the nucleus of the greatest Jewish community in the world today, a community of more than two millions.

The Constitution of 1787 proclaimed that religious denomination should play no part in determining a man's fitness for any official post in the United States.

Especially between the years 1881 and 1914, America was destined to be the great gathering ground for hundreds of thousands of refugees from the Jewish communities of eastern Europe, and in Hitler's time from both eastern and western Europe.

Today the Jewish population of the United States comprises more than five and a half million citizens out of a world total of twelve million Jews—the greatest and most significant *diaspora* in Jewish history.

After their liberation from the ghetto, the Jewish people's many talents made an immediate and tremendous impact in all spheres of culture and civilization. To list only a few of the innumerable creative personalities: in the sphere of figurative art (hitherto closed to them), there are the painters Camille Pissarro, Josef Israels, Max Liebermann, Amadeo Modigliani, Marc Chagall, and the sculptor Jacob Epstein. In literature and music, Ludwig Börne, Heinrich Heine, Hugo von Hofmannsthal, Arthur Schnitzler, Karl Kraus, Alfred Döblin, Stefan Zweig, Franz Kafka, Franz Werfel; among composers, Felix Mendelssohn-Bartholdy, Jacques Offenbach, Giacomo Meyerbeer, Gustav Mahler, Arnold Schönberg and Darius Milhaud, among conductors Bruno Walter and Otto Klemperer, and performers, Joseph Joachim, Artur Rubinstein, Bronislaw Hubermann, Artur Schnabel, and David Oistrakh.

The art of the theatre was given a new orientation by Max Reinhardt after the First World War. Among many other fine performers, we should mention Elisa Rachel and Sarah Bernhardt.

Vital contributions to science and philosophy have often been made by Jews. Albert Einstein founded the modern theory of relativity, revolutionizing man's cosmological and ideological outlook on life. Fritz Haber discovered the process for extracting ammonia from the air, thereby saving German agriculture during the First World War from what might have been a catastrophic shortage of fertilizer. In 1875 Siegfried Marcus built the first petrol-driven motor-car; the microphone was in-

WE ARE HERE
TO IMMORTALIZE THE DIVINE
IN THE HUMAN SPIRIT

Whoever sees the answer to the problem of history in economic or political materialism, whoever sees history, that is, as nothing more than a necessary struggle between economic or political or national powers, and regards the spiritual as something quite external to these events, will never be able to comprehend what Judaism signifies to humankind. For this reason neither a Karl Marx... nor a Heinrich von Treitschke... could understand Judaism.

From *Das Judentum* by Leo Baeck.

*

We are not here for the sake of possessions, nor for the sake of power, nor for the sake of happiness; we are here to immortalize the divine in the human spirit.

From *In Days to Come* by Walter Rathenau.

*

I never on my path have met the god with whom one wrestles till he blesses one.

From *The Fool and Death* by Hugo von Hofmannsthal.

*

The world into which man is born is senseless. Instinct and chance determine every course and reason, that fearful distinctive mark of humanity, stands confused by the brutal play of the elements.

For though involvement in the universal tragedy, the flaw, the guilt (hereditary guilt) is total, it is only the aware who atone.

From the foreword to Franz Werfel's German adaptation of Euripides' *The Trojan Women*.

*

And swaying, they walk in their clothes
On the gravel paths,
Beneath this great sky,
Spreading from distant hills
To hills in the distance.

From Franz Kafka: *Novellen, Skizzen, Aphorismen aus dem Nachlass*.

Introductory verse to the story *Beschreibung eines Kampfes*.

*

Angel of suppliants,
bless the sand,
that it may know the language of longing,
from which the new will grow as from a child's hand,
ever again the new!

From *Sternverdunkelung* by Nelly Sachs.

Albert Einstein (1879–1955) propounded the theory of relativity. He was professor at Zurich; from 1914 director of the Kaiser-Wilhelm-Institut für Physik in Berlin, and from 1933 professor at the Institute for Advanced Studies of Princeton University. His mass and energy equations formed the basis of modern scientific research.

Where wast thou when I laid the foundations of the earth? Declare, if thou hast understanding. Who hath laid the measures thereof, if thou knowest? or who laid the corner stone thereof; When the morning stars sang together, and all the sons of God shouted for joy? (From the Book of Job 38, 4–7)

Morning Star, painting by Ben Shahn, one of the important Jewish artists of America today.

vented by Emil Berliner and colour photography by Gabriel Lippmann. Pioneering work was done in medicine by Paul Ehrlich, co-founder of serum therapy and inventor of salvarsan; by August von Wassermann, famous for his Wassermann test; by Waldemar M. Haffkine, who discovered the virus of bubonic plague; by Sigmund Freud, founder of psychoanalysis, and Alfred Adler, exponent of individual psychology. In philosophy we have the Frenchman Henri Bergson and the Germans Hermann Cohen, Ernst Cassirer and Edmund Husserl.

During the nineteenth and twentieth centuries Jews played an active part in contemporary politics: Sir Moses Montefiore was Sheriff of London and financial adviser to Queen Victoria. He was a philanthropist always ready to help his oppressed co-religionists, not only with his great fortune but by direct diplomatic intervention, as, for example (together with Crémieux), with the Sultan of Constantinople, or Tsar Nicholas I in Moscow.

Isaac Adolphe Crémieux, French politician and finance minister, actively defended Jewish rights both inside France and, with Montefiore, in the Levant. As minister of justice he did away with slavery in the French colonies and abolished the death penalty for political crimes.

Benjamin Disraeli, Earl of Beaconsfield, was leader of the English Conservative Party and twice prime minister under Queen Victoria. Although baptized, he was always proud of his Jewish descent which he never sought to conceal.

In 1863 Ferdinand Lassalle founded the *Allgemeiner deutscher Arbeiterverein* (German General Workers' Union), the first workers' organization in the world. From it the German Social Democratic Party evolved.

Léon Blum, the leader of the French Socialist Party, was several times prime minister.

The great industrialist, banker and philosopher, Walter Rathenau, was foreign minister at the time of the Weimar Republic, and was murdered in 1922, because of his humanitarian and liberal views, by members of the fascist *Eberhardtbrigade*.

An honourable place is occupied by Jews in the American political and social scene: Bernard Baruch was (unofficial) adviser to American presidents from Wilson to Eisenhower. Herbert H. Lehman was four times governor of New York since 1928, and later became a senator. Joseph Pulitzer as founder of the *New York World* and Adolph S. Ochs as publisher of the *New York Times* are largely responsible for the high standing of American journalism.

The tremendous development that took place during the nineteenth century in the field of industry and communications demanded ready capital and the financing of new enterprises on a scale never known before. It was here that the Jewish economic genius found its true vocation. One need only recall names such as Rothschild, Bleichröder, Wertheimer, or Sassoon. They founded whole family dynasties with complex international connections. The House of Rothschild has rightly been called the sixth great power of Europe. Ministers, ambassadors and heads of government were their habitual guests.

With the development of government financial institutions at the beginning of the twentieth century the importance of private banks waned. Jews took their place in industry and commerce and played an important part in the development of new forms of economy, such as cartels, limited companies, cooperatives, consumer groups and department stores, as well as of modern mass production.

The emancipation of the European and American Jews resulted in greatly increased assimilation with their Christian surroundings. Freed from the narrowness of the ghetto and from the fetters of traditional teaching, many of them—the number is estimated at two hundred thousand—broke with their own tradition and had themselves baptized. Others sought religious comfort in the newly founded Reform movement of which the originators are Abraham Geiger and Samuel Holdheim.

While ancient orthodoxy was no longer in a position to establish communication with so fundamentally changed a world and continued to base its dogma on medieval tradition, the Reform movement was able to introduce certain relaxations, such as the transfer of the Sabbath service to Sunday. The schism between orthodoxy and Reform Judaism has not so far been healed and remains a grave problem for the future of Judaism.

The exceptional flowering of European and American Jewry in the nineteenth and twentieth centuries brought about a sharp rise in population. It is believed that at the time of the destruction of the second Temple and the beginning of the *diaspora* Jews numbered some four and a half millions, a figure which, by the twelfth century, had declined to two millions. Up till the seventeenth century it varied between one and a half and two millions and by 1800 had risen to two and a half millions. In the nineteenth century there was a rapid increase to ten and a half millions by 1900. On the outbreak of the Second World War this figure had risen to sixteen millions in the whole of the western hemisphere. After the catastrophe of the National Socialist extermination campaign this had fallen to ten millions.

Martin Buber (1878–1965), came of a Galician family of scholars. From 1930–33 he was professor of Jewish religious philosophy and ethics at the University of Frankfurt am Main, and from 1938 professor of social philosophy at the Hebrew University of Jerusalem. He became the interpreter of the Jewish faith and the young generation the world over looked to him for guidance.

REAPPRAISAL

The scientific and historical spirit of the nineteenth century had a tremendous effect on the Jews. It led to a kind of reappraisal of their own past and their own values, and to the founding of the 'Science of Judaism'. Its most important historian was Heinrich Graetz (1817–91), who wrote a monumental Jewish history in German which is still the standard work. Another important historian was Simon Dubnow (1860–1941), whose history of the Jewish people was written in Russian with stress mainly on eastern Jewry. Twentieth-century representatives of the Science of Judaism were Leo Baeck, the Chief Rabbi of German Jewry, and Martin Buber, the wise and percipient scholar of Hasidism and the Jewish tradition whose religious-philosophical works exerted enormous influence upon both Jewish and non-Jewish thought.

The liberal ideas of the nineteenth century took far longer to penetrate into Poland and Russia, and the Jewish communities there were much less affected by them. Yet even so they brought into being a movement known as *Haskalah* or enlightenment, and there was a flowering of secular literature in Hebrew and Yiddish. The centre of Yiddish literature was no longer the rabbi or hasid, but the simple Jew of the people. The world of eastern Jewry found a lasting memorial in the works of its chief poets.

The era of reappraisal led individual thinkers to recognize the abnormal position of the Jewish people in the *diaspora*. A pamphlet by Leo Pinsker written in 1882 and called *Auto-emancipation* emphatically declares that the Jewish people must take their fate into their own hands, an undertaking possible only when they were established in their own ancestral territory, the Holy Land. Its effect was tremendous.

A generation earlier Moses Hess, in his book *Rome and Jerusalem* (1862), had expressed similar ideas.

The dawning realization of their true situation led to the formation of *Hoveve Zion,* the society of the Friends of Zion. It aimed at the settlement of its members in Palestine, where they became the first agricultural settlers.

In the strongest contrast to the Iranian conception with all its later ramifications, the Jewish conception is that the happenings of this world take place not in the sphere between two principles, light and darkness, or good and evil, but in the sphere between God and men, these mortal, brittle human beings who yet are able to face God and withstand his word.

From *The Faith of Judaism* by Martin Buber.

ZIONISM

Theodor Herzl (1860–1904), author, correspondent of the *Neue Freie Presse*, of Vienna. Shattered by the Dreyfus trial in Paris (1894), Herzl, a Jew who had been fully assimilated, became the founder of modern political Zionism. His life was devoted to this task.

No one is strong or rich enough to transplant a people from one home to another. Only an idea can do that. The idea of a state has this power. Throughout the night of their history, Jews have never ceased to dream the royal dream: 'Next year in Jerusalem!' It is our old saying. Now it is a matter of showing that dream can become an idea in daylight clarity.

From *Der Judenstaat* by Theodor Herzl.

Western Jewry, content to see in the emancipation of the nineteenth century the final solution of the Jewish question, took little interest in the idea of a return to the Holy Land. They dismissed it with condescension, until circumstances led them to think otherwise.

Theodor Herzl, editor of the *Neue Freie Presse* in Vienna, was so shattered by the impact of the Dreyfus affair in Paris in 1894, which he witnessed in his capacity as correspondent, that he became the founder of political Zionism. He was a completely assimilated Jew and had for a time intended to have his children baptized.

1896 saw the appearance of his book *The Jewish State* which for the first time clearly formulated proposals for the setting up of a political commonwealth of Jewish people in the Holy Land. In 1897 he summoned the first Zionist Congress in Basle whose two hundred delegates formulated the aim of the movement in the 'Basle Programme': 'to create for the Jewish people a home in Palestine secured by public law.'

The following years were taken up with travelling between the courts and governments of Europe—Constantinople, London, Paris, Berlin—where he sought to gain friends for the cause of Zionism, and to come to an agreement with the Sultan, in whose dominion Palestine lay, regarding the settlement of Jews.

His diplomatic efforts resulted in England's consenting to a Jewish settlement area in Kenya in British East Africa. It was one of the great disappointments of his life that this proposal, known as the Uganda Plan, was rejected by the sixth Zionist Congress, the loudest dissentient voices being those of the Polish and Russian delegates.

Herzl, driven by a mystical faith in his mission and exhausted by his ceaseless Zionist activities, died in 1904 at the early age of forty-four.

The central figure in Zionism after his death was Chaim Weizmann, professor of chemistry at the University of Manchester. As a supporter of practical Zionism, he was responsible for setting up the Jewish National Fund, with the object of purchasing land in Palestine to be the inalienable property of the Jewish people.

In 1870 the work of settlement had begun, characteristically enough, with the founding of an agricultural college at Mikve Israel near Jaffa by the *Alliance Israélite Universelle*, the philanthropic organization of French Jewry.

The agricultural settlements that were founded as a result, such as Motza near Jerusalem, Petah Tikvah (gate of hope), Rishon le Zion (first in Zion), Rehovot and Zikhron Ya'akov, were all laid out along the lines of a European village, though some of them were surrounded by a wall as a protection against hostile Bedouin.

These early settlers, mostly belonging to the *Hoveve Zion* movement, had a very hard time of it. Without agricultural experience, in hostile surroundings, in an unfavourable climate and occupying a malarial area, they would certainly have come to grief had it not been for the Baron Edmond de Rothschild of Paris. He gave them financial support, bought their produce, especially the wine of Zikhron Ya'akov and Rishon le Zion, and sent them agricultural advisers. These early settlements are today flourishing villages, or else have grown into towns.

Between 1904 and 1914 a wave of immigrants reached Palestine known as the Second Aliyah, or immigration into the Holy Land. With it came a new type of settler, mostly young intellectuals influenced by modern democratic and socialist ideas who were prepared to sacrifice studies and professions in Europe in order to develop the land. The Second Aliyah brought in most of those who would later be the country's leading political personalities, such as David Ben Gurion or the present prime minister, Levi Eshkol.

In 1909, a group of workers combined to work communally a piece of land near the Jordan effluent from Lake Gennesaret which had been put at their disposal by the National Fund. They called their settlement Deganya. It was the first of those agricultural communal settlements known as *kibbutzim*.

In the same year the inhabitants of Jaffa founded the first completely Jewish town, Jaffa's 'garden suburb' among the sand dunes, and called it Tel Aviv, 'Hill of Spring'.

At the outbreak of the First World War some one hundred thousand Jews were living in Palestine, fifty thousand in Jerusalem, and twelve thousand in the agricultural settlements. At the end of the war the figure had declined to sixty thousand.

Turkey fought on the side of the Germans. Under Kemal Pasha, the country was subjected to an oppressive reign of terror.

In 1917 the British army commanded by General Allenby began driving out the Turkish forces, and for the first time in almost two thousand years Jewish-Palestinian units fought for their own country beside the English during the mopping-up operations in the autumn of 1918.

Weizmann's diplomatic efforts and those of his colleagues Ussishkin, Sokolov and Tchlenov during the war succeeded in obtaining from the British government an expression of sympathy for the setting up of a homeland for the Jewish people in Palestine: this was the Balfour Declaration of 2 November 1917, a letter from the British foreign minister, Lord Balfour, to Lord Rothschild.

Although it does not contain any binding political commitment on the part of the British government towards the Jews, and is so formulated as to permit a number of interpretations, it was still the first official expression of sympathy by a major power for the efforts of the Zionist movement and a promise to facilitate as far as possible the establishment of a national home. It must be regarded as a milestone along the road of the Jewish people's return to their country.

On 25 April 1920 at the San Remo peace conference, England was entrusted by the League of Nations with the mandate over Palestine and Transjordan for the future national home of the Jews. The first High Commissioner of the mandatory government was a Jew, Sir Herbert Samuel.

To a large extent the Jews evolved their own autonomous authorities, the chief of which was the *Vaad Leumi* or National Council. Connections were maintained with world Jewry through the Jewish Agency for Palestine which was founded in 1929 and consisted of both Zionists and non-Zionists. It represented world Jewry in the face of the Palestine mandate government. Hence, on the one hand, the latter found itself confronted by the well-organized *Yishuv*, or Jewish population, with its own body of opinion, and on the other by an anonymous mass of Arabs hostile to any form of organization and ruled by a number of rich and mutually competitive *effendis*. From the beginning the Jewish sector was thus a state within a state, whereas with the Arab sector, the administration was in direct and sustained relation.

The Arab population, stirred up by political and religious agitators, showed no understanding at all of Britain's Palestine policy, and there were fierce uprisings in

Chaim Weizmann (1874–1952) was born in Motol near Pinsk in Poland. His career began at Manchester University as professor of organic chemistry; his synthetic production of acetone was of great importance in the manufacture of explosives. Because of this valuable contribution to England's military success, he was held in high esteem by the British government. Weizmann, one of the most important representatives of practical Zionism, was largely responsible for starting the Jewish National Fund towards the purchase of land in Palestine, which has been in operation since 1909. As leader of the English Zionists, he brought about the Balfour Declaration in 1917. In 1918, Weizmann laid the foundation stone of the Hebrew University in Jerusalem. He was the founder of the Weizmann Institute for Biochemistry and Nuclear Research. Weizmann was the first president of the State of Israel.

Nahalal in the valley of Jezreel, the first *moshav* (co-operative settlement) in the country, was founded in 1921.

While in a kibbutz (communal settlement) the land is worked by everyone in common, each individual settler family in a moshav has its own allotted and equal share of the land. But in a moshav, as in a kibbutz, the land is the inalienable property of the nation.

In 1933, Anne Frank and her family had to leave Germany. The small Jewish family found refuge in Holland, and were eventually hidden by their protectors in the back premises of a house on Prinsengracht in Amsterdam, while the danger grew greater day by day.

Anne, a gifted, precocious thirteen-year-old, saw the sufferings of this small clandestine group of Jewish people as part of the fate of her nation awaiting its deliverance. She never gave up her heroic decision to survive the horror, sustained always by the fervent hope for an ideal future when she could live as a human being without stigma.

'Tuesday, 11 April 1944.

... Then a quarter past eleven, a bustle and noise downstairs. Everyone's breath was audible, otherwise no one moved. Footsteps in the house, in the private office, kitchen, then... on our staircase. No one breathed audibly now, footsteps on our staircase, then a rattle of the revolving cupboard. This moment is indescribable. "Now we are lost!" I thought, and could see us all being taken away by the Gestapo that very night. Twice they rattled at the cupboard, then there was nothing, the footsteps withdrew, we were saved so far. A shiver seemed to pass from one to another, I heard someone's teeth chattering, no one said a word.... We have been pointedly reminded that we are in hiding, that we are Jews in chains, chained to one spot, without any rights, but with a thousand duties. We Jews mustn't show our feelings, must be brave and strong, must accept our fate and not grumble, must do what is within our power and trust in God. Sometime this terrible war will be over. Surely the time will come when we are people again, and not just Jews. Who has inflicted this upon us? Who has made us Jews different to all other people? Who has allowed us to suffer so terribly up till now? It is

1920, 1921 and between 1936 and 1939 which were met by the Yishuv with remarkable restraint and discipline.

The mandatory government laid down a yearly immigration quota. Whereas at the time of the Balfour Declaration the Jewish population numbered about 60,000, by the outbreak of the Second World War it had risen to something like half a million. In rural areas there were 270 agricultural settlements with 143,000 inhabitants of which 40,000 lived in kibbutzim. Tel Aviv had grown into a modern city with nearly 150,000 inhabitants.

Development in the intellectual field had been important. An unremitting advocate of Hebrew was Eliezer Ben Jehuda, and poets and authors like Chaim Nachman Bialik, Saul Tchernichovski, Ahad Ha-Am (otherwise Asher Ginzberg) and Abraham Shlonsky also gave it a tremendous impulse. The incomparable achievement of the Jewish renaissance is the revival of the language of the Bible and its adaptation to the world of today.

In 1925 in Jerusalem on Mount Scopus, and in the presence of Lord Balfour, the university was inaugurated. Instruction is given in Hebrew.

A Hebrew theatre came into being, the *Habimah*, which won international recognition.

In 1936 the Palestine Philharmonic Orchestra founded by Bronislaw Hubermann, the world-famous violonist, gave its first concert under Toscanini.

THE 'FINAL SOLUTION OF THE JEWISH QUESTION'

The era of emancipation and equal rights had checked outbreaks of anti-Jewish feeling, once more to raise its head in the form of modern racial anti-Semitism and of Adolf Hitler's National Socialist movement, for the doctrine of the racial enemy is an integral part of National Socialism.

The National Socialist German Workers Party (NSDAP) was formed in Munich in 1920. From the beginning Hitler and his henchmen made their strong anti-Semitic attitude all too plain. The *Protocols of the Elders of Zion*—one of the greatest historical forgeries of all time, of which millions of copies were distributed by the Nazis— alleged that the object of the Jewish people was world hegemony, and every means must be used to combat them.

Hitler was appointed chancellor on 30 January 1933, obtained almost unlimited power through the Enabling Act of 24 March 1933, and by 1 April had already instituted the official anti-Jewish terror. A little later Jews were evicted from government service, from the judiciary and from the universities. By the Nuremberg Laws of 1935 they were deprived of citizenship, and marriage between Germans and Jews was forbidden. The next step was to exclude them from commerce, the theatre, art, and every kind of cultural activity.

Organized riots and 'spontaneous' excesses reached their climax in the 'crystal night' of 9/10 November 1938. Hundreds of synagogues were burnt down, and innumerable Jewish businesses looted and destroyed.

It is hard to understand how the world could react with indifference to these barbaric pogroms, and that nowhere was any voice raised in effective protest.

Of the original 600,000 German Jews, some 350,000 escaped during the first six years.

On 1 September 1939 the German army invaded Poland. The war had begun. Jews were concentrated in the *Gouvernement Général* near Lublin and in ghettos in large towns such as Warsaw, Lodz, Cracow, Lemberg and Vilna, so as to be easily accessible for forced labour. Many hundreds of thousands died from exhaustion and starvation.

After the attack on the Soviet Union in 1941, Jewish persecution entered a new and final phase. Special commando units of the SS and the police—'task forces'—were formed, to follow in the wake of the army in order to 'liquidate' Jews and political commissars in the conquered territories. In that same year the task forces went into operation between the Baltic and the Black Sea, where 350,000 Jews fell victim to their mass executions and pogroms.

In the autumn of 1941 there began the first deportations from within the Reich to ghettos and concentration camps in the east.

And now, in 1942, the 'final solution' came into operation. The Wannsee Protocol describes a conference on 20 January 1942 in Berlin-Wannsee, at which Heydrich gave instructions to members of the SS and the police for the physical extermination of German Jewry. What took place after this in the extermination camps of Auschwitz, Belsen, Chelmno, Sobibor, Treblinka and Maidanek is beyond all human belief.

Of the 500,000 Jews who were herded together in the Warsaw ghetto, 40,000 remained in 1943. When it was their turn to be transported to extermination camps, they put up a desperate resistance against the German garrison. The rebellion lasted thirty-six days. Nothing remained of the ghetto but smoking rubble. Only a few succeeded in making their way through the network of sewage canals to join the Polish partisans.

The total number of Jews murdered by the National Socialists was 5,700,000, half the Jewish population of Europe and more than a third of the total Jewish population of the world.

It was the greatest catastrophe that had ever befallen the Jewish people.

END OF MANDATE RULE

All escape routes from Europe were blocked. There was one last chance in the Balkans, where Hitler's forces were thin on the ground. It was from there that young Jews organized illegal emigration to Palestine. It had to remain illegal, since it was irreconcilable with the immigration quota laid down by the mandatory government.

On 17 May 1939, the British government under Neville Chamberlain issued a White Paper recommending the virtual suppression of immigration and land purchase. At the time of the worst crisis ever experienced by European Jewry, the recommendations of the White Paper were in direct opposition to British undertakings and they represented a heavy blow to the Jews of Palestine.

When the Labour Party took office at the end of the Second World War, it seemed reasonable to expect that the Palestine mandate would be honoured; it had been one of the points in the programme of the opposition. But the decisions of 1939 remained

God that has made us as we are, but it will be God, too, who will raise us up again. If we bear all this suffering and if there are still Jews left, when it is over, then Jews, instead of being doomed, will be held up as an example. Who knows, it might even be our religion from which the world and all peoples learn good, and for that reason, and that reason only, do we have to suffer now... God has never deserted our people. Right through the ages there have been Jews, through all the ages they have had to suffer, but it has made them strong too; the weak fall, but the strong will remain and never go under!...

Saturday, 15 July 1944.

... It's really a miracle that I haven't dropped all my ideals because they seem so absurd and impossible to carry out. Yet I keep them, because in spite of everything I still believe that people are really good at heart. I simply can't build up my hopes on a foundation consisting of confusion, misery, and death. I see the world gradually being turned into a wilderness, I hear the ever-approaching thunder, which will destroy us too, I can feel the sufferings of millions and yet, if I look up into the heavens, I think that it will all come right, that this cruelty too will end, and that peace and tranquillity will return again.
In the meantime, I must uphold my ideals, for perhaps the time will come when I shall be able to carry them out....'

On 4 August 1944 the Gestapo irrupted into the back premises, arrested all those in hiding and put them into concentration camps.

Anne Frank died in March 1945 in the Bergen-Belsen concentration camp, two months before the liberation of Holland.

In July 1947 the Haganah chartered the *President Warfield*, a small ship 320 feet long. As *Exodus 47*, she was to carry several thousand Jewish refugees to Palestine. The ship left without official English sanction during the night 12/13 July; she carried water and provisions for a week, and 4,554 passengers instead of the 700 for which she had been built. Five British destroyers shadowed her, and when they judged she had entered Palestinian territorial waters she was intercepted and boarded. In Haifa harbour, the passengers were transferred to three 'liberty ships' behind barbed wire and

were transported, not to the usual clearing centre in Cyprus—the official reason being that accommodation could not be found for four thousand people—but to France where they lay at anchor for twenty-four days. Here the Jews stood firm in their resolve not to leave the ship alive except to land in Palestine, so that the British government determined that they must be sent back to Germany. Thirty days later, instead of arriving in the Promised Land, the refugees ended up at Poppendorf camp, seven miles from Lübeck.

in force and the policy of the new foreign minister, Ernest Bevin, was deliberately anti-Jewish.

Three times President Truman proposed an act of clemency: a hundred thousand survivors of concentration camps should, immediately and unconditionally, be permitted to enter the country. The proposal was thrice rejected.

The answer of the Yishuv to the White Paper recommendations was to continue illegal immigration and also passive and active resistance to the mandatory government.

In the affairs of the ships *Struma, Patria* and *Exodus,* illegal immigration had tragic consequences. In 1939 the *Struma* lay off Constantinople for two and a half months with eight hundred refugees on board and, because of British pressure, was unable to get permission either to sail or to enter a Turkish port. Finally the unseaworthy ship sailed back into the Black Sea where she foundered with the whole of her unfortunate human cargo. Only one passenger survived as witness of the disaster.

During the attempt to stop refugees landing at the port of Haifa from the *Patria,* a bomb exploded on board the ship and 250 people lost their lives.

The 4,500 'displaced persons' on board the *Exodus* in 1947 were escorted into Haifa by British warships, whence, to the horror of the whole world, they were shipped back to former camps in Germany.

Force of circumstance had brought into existence terrorist organizations whose retributive acts, such as the assassination of Lord Moyne in Egypt, and the demolition of a wing of the King David Hotel, British GHQ in Jerusalem, killing ninety British government officials, were not condoned by the majority of Jews in the country.

The Jewish population, in spite of intense psychological stress, behaved with admirable moderation, but the *Haganah,* an armed organization for self-defence against Arab attack, was responsible for repeated acts of sabotage against military installations and objectives of strategic importance.

In spite of the mandatory government's unsympathetic policy, many Jews volunteered to help the British war effort. Towards the end of the war a Jewish Brigade was fighting the Germans in northern Italy; when the war was over, the Brigade cared for many displaced persons in Italy, endeavouring to relieve their lot.

A group of Jews experienced in guerilla tactics were dropped by the RAF behind German lines to carry out acts of sabotage and to send back information. The names of Hannah Senesh, a young student, and Enzo Sireni, an Italian Jew, member of the Givat Brenner kibbutz, will never be forgotten.

When the tension at last became intolerable, the British government decided in April 1947 to place the Palestine problem before the newly formed United Nations Organization.

A commission of investigation with members of eleven different nationalities—it was to be the last of many—recommended the partition of the country into a Jewish and an Arab state. Jerusalem was to be made international and placed under the direct control of the United Nations. President Truman's suggestion to admit 100,000 displaced persons was endorsed.

On 29 November 1947 the full assembly of the United Nations, by more than the required two-thirds majority, ratified the plan for the partition of the country.

The Jews gave their consent. But the Arab states rejected the decision to which they responded by attacks on the Jewish population.

While bloody rioting was still going on, England declared that she was not in a position to carry out the recommendations of the United Nations and announced that she would give up her mandate; on 15 May 1948 she withdrew her forces.

ISRAEL—THE NEW STATE

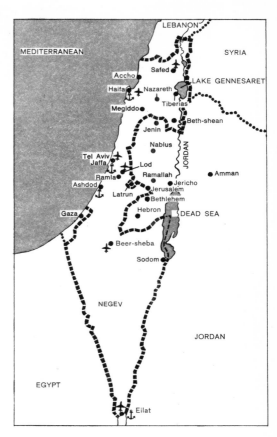

Israel—the new state (1949 armistice frontiers).

On 14 May 1948 at four in the afternoon, before the termination at midnight of the British mandate over Palestine, David Ben Gurion proclaimed in Tel Aviv the sovereign state of ISRAEL in the area prescribed by the United Nations. Chaim Weizmann became Israel's first president, Ben Gurion prime minister of the provisional government, and Jerusalem the capital city of the new state.

The last signature on the declaration of independence had barely had time to dry or the final note of the national anthem to die away before the first Egyptian aircraft appeared over the city. Thus there was open war between the Israelis and the forces of the Arab League. The armies of seven Arab states were on the march, their purpose to rescind the United Nations' decision on partition and so to prevent by force of arms the formation of an independent Jewish state.

Even before this, when the mandatory power was still responsible for peace and order in Palestine, and despite the presence of strong British forces, Arab irregulars had raided Jewish settlements and carried out attacks on lines of communication. Jewish defensive organizations, the Haganah and the extremist group, the *Irgun Tzevai Leumi,* had struck back, as far as their meagre military equipment allowed. The approaches to Jerusalem presented a special problem, as they led through mountainous country held by Arabs.

But 14 May, even though it had brought about attack by regular, well-equipped Arab armies, did at least mean that Jewish defence forces could for the first time officially import arms and constitute themselves an army. Previously, *Haganah* and *Irgun* had been forced by the British into the underground and their weapons had often been confiscated. Now the earlier extremist organizations amalgamated with the Haganah to become the *Tzeva Haganah le-Israel,* and within a short time, with the help of arms from Czechoslovakia, the Israeli Army had become a strong and efficient fighting force.

In the first phase of the fighting, the newly formed army succeeded in holding most of the Jewish areas of settlement, until the four weeks' armistice imposed by the Security Council of the United Nations came into force on 11 June. When on 8 July the Arab states opposed its renewal, Israel went over to counter-attack and improved her strategic position by the capture of Lydda, Ramla and Nazareth, before the Arabs agreed to another armistice.

Only the Arab Legion of Transjordan, under the command of British officers, had succeeded in occupying any appreciable area of Palestine, including the Old City of Jerusalem. Legionaries also held the town of Latrun against all Israeli onslaughts, so that the approach road to Jerusalem was cut and the hundred thousand Jews in the Holy City found themselves in a critical position. The besieged town was enabled to hold out only by the construction of a by-pass.

David Ben Gurion, born in 1886 in Plonsk (Poland), came to the country in 1906 where he became co-founder of the Socialist Zionist Party (Poale Zion). Expelled by the Turks in 1915, he returned in 1918. It was largely through his initiative that the General Federation of Labour (Histadrut) came into being,

with Ben Gurion as its General Secretary. He was responsible for directing the newly founded Labour Party (Mapai) as also, after 1935, the Jewish Agency for Palestine. After the founding of the State of Israel (14 May 1948), Ben Gurion became the first prime minister and minister of defence, posts which he held at intervals until 1963. Ben Gurion, still Israel's most eminent political personality, now puts all his energy into serving his country as a member of Parliament (Knesset).

The Egyptian Army which, at the beginning of the war, had advanced to within thirty miles of Tel Aviv, was forced to retreat. During the second armistice, in spite of clear and definite terms, it refused to permit the passage of food convoys to the Jewish settlement in the Negev; Israel again resorted to arms, overran the Egyptian positions in southern Palestine including the desert capital, Beersheba, and so gained control of that region which represents not only the country's great land reserve but also contains the port of Eilat on the Gulf of Aqaba, through which Israel conducts her commerce with Asia and East Africa. Shortly afterwards, the last of the Arab irregulars were driven out of Galilee.

Armistice negotiations began almost immediately in Rhodes, presided over by the UN mediator Ralph J. Bunche. Egypt was the first Arab state to sign the armistice agreement on 24 February 1949; Libya, (Trans-)Jordan and Syria came next. The area occupied by Israel was extended northwards to include Galilee, and the Negev desert in the south. But the partition of Jerusalem, giving the Old City to Jordan and the New to Israel was a decision not only incomprehensible but also hurtful to Jewish sentiment. Jordan also acquired the towns of Jenin, Nablus (the Biblical Sichem), Ramallah, Jericho, Bethlehem and Hebron. England, the United States and France undertook to guarantee the agreed frontiers.

The new state had successfully withstood her first military test and at the same time had consolidated her diplomatic position. Israel had received international *de jure* recognition. On the very day of its proclamation, the President of the United States had announced its recognition *de facto,* as not long afterwards did another great power, Russia.

Before the armistice negotiations were over, the first parliamentary elections had taken place on 25 January 1949, and the 120 delegates of the *Knesset* (the Jewish parliament) in turn elected the first government of the state of Israel.

Israel was now able to begin to fulfil the mission for which she had been created —the provision of a homeland for homeless Jews. The survivors of the National Socialist régime need no longer wait in camps in Europe, or risk being kept away from Palestinian shores by the Royal Navy.

After 15 May 100,000 Jews entered Israel in 1948 alone; in 1949 the figure was 240,000. In a few years the population had grown by more than two millions. Besides the 'displaced persons' from Europe, immigrants were mainly Jews from Arab countries brought to Israel by the war of liberation. Their number equalled that of Arab refugees leaving Israel, so that in effect there was an exchange of populations.

Mass immigration presented the country with immeasurable problems. The desert was made fruitful, industry was developed, the small amount of mineral deposits exploited. New towns arose in the desert, and after the first difficult years of privation and austerity the new immigrants, and with them their country, have achieved a standard of living which is slowly but steadily catching up on that of Europe.

To these economic problems was added the great task of forging a single people with a common national Hebrew culture out of immigrants from a hundred different countries with greatly varying cultural backgrounds and all speaking different languages.

In spite of the friction inevitable between such marked ethnic groups, the process of 'becoming a people' was reasonably rapid. After two thousand years of dispersion all over the world, years of persecution, of oppression and expulsion, years of contempt, of hatred and of unspeakable suffering, the Jewish people once again became masters of their own destiny in their Promised Land.

THE SYMBOL OF REDEMPTION

A star of David, here between rosettes ornamenting a frieze of the Kefar Nahum synagogue, third century A.D.

The story of the star of David and its significance in Jewry goes back to the world of Jewish magic before the sixth century after Christ. The six-pointed star, the hexagram, and often the pentagram also, served as a magic sign, a talisman against demons. This was essentially its meaning to most people until the first half of the nineteenth century; it was never a real symbol of Judaism like the menorah, the seven-branched candelabrum. The term 'star of David' or 'shield of David' was not used in respect of the hexagram in Hebrew literature until the thirteenth century; there is nothing to indicate how the symbol originally acquired the name. After the seventeenth century, under the influence of the Kabbalah, the star of David became a symbol of the vision of Messianic redemption. At about the same time the hexagram began to be used 'officially' as the mark of a Jewish community; the custom originated in Prague.

The fathers of the Zionist movement adopted it as the national emblem at the Basle Congress in 1897. 'The star of David owed its sanctification as a national emblem much less to Zionism, however, than to those who turned it into a badge of humiliation and shame for millions of people. The yellow Jewish star, sign of ostracism and eventual annihilation, accompanied the Jews on their journey of degradation and horror, and in their struggle and heroic resistance. Under this sign they were murdered; under this sign they came to Israel.' (Gershom Scholem.)

A MATTER OF LIFE AND DEATH: THE SIX-DAY WAR

Deliver me, O Lord,
from the evil man:
preserve me
from the violent man:
which imagine mischiefs
in their heart;
continually are they
gathered together for war.
They have sharpened
their tongues
like a serpent;
adders' poison is under
their lips.

(PSALM 140, 1–4)

David Ben Gurion, the great organizer of the Jewish state, was able to steer the ship of state successfully across stormy waters and in between reefs, but no safe political anchorage was available in foreign affairs. The Arab states refused to recognize Israel and were not prepared to treat for peace. Terrorist gangs along the frontiers maintained a condition of perpetual disturbance. Because the UN Security Council was powerless, Israel had recourse to isolated retaliatory measures of which the most important—the Sinai campaign against Egypt in October 1956—brought the whole of the Sinai peninsula into her hands within a week. She was deprived of the political advantage of her victory by American intervention and the threat of sanctions, which compelled her to withdraw. The hope of peace with her neighbours remained unfulfilled. Shortly after Israel had celebrated her nineteenth birthday in 1967, the situation in the Near East once more became suddenly critical. The extreme left-wing régime in Damascus had for some time been the leader of the Arab activists and had used the region adjoining Israel to the north as a base for terrorist organizations, intending to unleash a 'popular war' by continual raids across the frontier. At the same time the Syrians accused President Gamal Abdel Nasser of being insufficiently aggressive towards the Zionist 'arch-enemy'. When the Security Council of the United Nations, their hands tied by the Soviet veto, failed to do anything about the Syrian inroads, Israel again took steps on her own. In aerial combat Israeli Mirages shot down six Syrian MIG's, and bombed Syrian positions without Nasser coming to the assistance of his fellow Arab state. But Syria was not daunted. Further terrorist acts were met with grave warnings, whereupon the Soviet Union, protector of Nasser and left-wing socialist régimes of the Near East, induced the Egyptians to invade the Sinai peninsula in full strength so as to prevent further retaliatory action by Israel in the north. But Nasser went too far. He demanded that the UN forces stationed in the Gaza Strip and in Sharm el-Sheikh (at the entrance to the Gulf of Aqaba) since after the Sinai war in 1957 be withdrawn; this the Secretary General of the United Nations, U Thant, did not hesitate to concede; Nasser then blockaded Eilat by closing the Straits of Tiran.

Israel declared repeatedly that she regarded this measure as a *casus belli*. But first an attempt was made to deflect Egypt from her warlike course by diplomatic methods. While Washington made vain efforts to organize the sea powers in common action or in a demand for the free passage of shipping, Nasser proclaimed a 'Holy War' in which the Jewish state was doomed to immediate destruction. When Hussein, Jordan's more moderate ruler who had been branded some days before by Nasser as a 'traitor to the Arab cause', did a dramatic about-turn and flew to Cairo for a reconciliation, even placing his own forces under the command of an Egyptian general, the noose was truly laid about the neck of Israel. It was a noose that the Jewish state, if she wished to survive, must sever before the knot was slipped.

On 5 June, Israel struck. Although the armies had been facing one another in a state of complete readiness for a fortnight, the impossible happened—Israel's sur-

Stage of the Six-Day War and the areas occupied by Israel after the fighting.

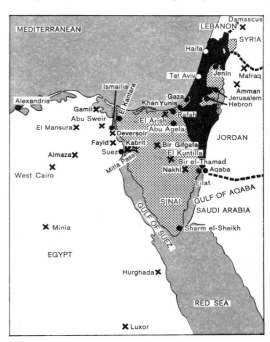

Israel's six-day campaign: On the morning of 5 June 1967, at 7.45, the Israeli air-force set out to strike a decisive blow against Egypt and her allies. After only a few hours the major part of the Egyptian, Jordanian, Syrian and Iraqi aircraft had been destroyed on the ground (Arab air bases marked on the map with a cross), and the opposing air-forces had thus been almost completely neutralized. At the same time Israel had begun ground operations at 8 a.m. with a massive armoured attack on Khan Yunis so as to seal off the Gaza Strip and to free their line of advance along the Rafah-El Arish-El Kantara railway. On the Jordanian front, the Israelis pushed forward towards Jenin, Latrun and Jerusalem.

During the early morning of the second day's fighting Jenin and Latrun fell into Israeli hands, and Ramallah shortly afterwards. Gaza, Rafah and El Arish were taken. Meanwhile two more spearheads went into action; one central armoured column pushed forward to Abu Agela from which they were to move on to Ismailia along the desert road, and a southern column went towards El Kuntilla, pushing on from there to the middle of the peninsula to reach the Suez Canal through the Mitla Pass. These operations went according to plan. At the same time motorized units began to advance along the Gulf of Aqaba in the direction of Sharm el-Sheikh.

The following day, 7 June, the Israelis in a pincer movement captured Nablus in Jordan, and occupied Jericho, Hebron and Bethlehem. After fierce street fighting, the Old City of Jerusalem was taken at 10.15. That evening Jordan declared its readiness for an armistice. In the Sinai peninsula the central column had reached Bir Gifgafa. There it split up, one section pressing on westwards towards Ismailia, the other goint to meet the units to the north which were advancing from El Arish to El Kantara which they reached towards evening. In the south, Israeli armoured units from El Kuntilla were approaching the Mitla Pass. Eventually Sharm el-Sheikh fell to the Israeli troops and air-borne contingents without putting up a fight—the Egyptians had already retreated. The blockade of the Gulf of Aqaba had been broken. On the Syrian front, however, ground fighting was just beginning.

After bitter fighting near Gifgafa and on the Mitla Pass, the Israeli army, by the fourth day, commanded the principal routes to the Canal Zone. Soon the Egyptians who had been surrounded in the Gaza Strip also capitulated. On this same evening of 8 June, Egypt accepted the UN order for a cease-fire.

On the northern front the Israelis struck with full force on the fifth day of war, capturing the commanding elevated positions on the Syrian-Israeli border in fierce fighting with heavy losses on both sides. Israeli units advanced to within fourteen miles of Damascus.

Fighting was still going on in Syria on 10 June. But towards evening there was an armistice in this sector too.

After the Six-Day War, Israeli troops held the Suez Canal, the Jordan and the most important road junctions on the route to Damascus; they controlled an area three times the size of Israel.

prise tactics succeeded. During the initial hours of the war, her aircraft destroyed most of Nasser's aircraft and most of those of Iraq, Syria and Jordan on the ground. In four days the Egyptian army in Sinai had been utterly defeated and the blockade of the Gulf of Aqaba lifted.

At the start of the war Israel had sent messages to King Hussein of Jordan inviting him to refrain from taking part in the war. His only reply was the Jordanian artillery's murderous shelling of the New City of Jerusalem and the suburbs of Tel Aviv. The Israeli army therefore had no choice but to proceed against Jordan. The areas formerly in Palestine which had been given to Hussein's grandfather Abdullah in 1948 were occupied. The most dramatic moment of the war, deeply moving even to non-religious Jews, was the capture of the Old City of Jerusalem. For the first time in nineteen years, Jews again had access to the Wailing Wall. For the first time the president of the independent Jewish state prayed before this great sanctuary of his people.

In the final hours of the Six-Day War, the Israelis stormed the little 'Maginot-line' on the north frontier, the fortified Syrian mountain ranges from which for two decades they had sniped at the agricultural settlements of the Hule Plain and the fishermen on Lake Tiberias.

After their life and death struggle, Israeli forces were stationed beside the Suez Canal, along the Jordan and at the most important road junctions leading to Damascus; the territory captured is three times the size of Israel. Defence minister Moshe Dayan, the victor of the Sinai campaign, was acclaimed as Israel's saviour for the second time; but the architect of the Six-Day War was Major-General Rabin.

It was not as it had been after the Sinai campaign. In the United Nations there was no majority demanding the unconditional withdrawal of Israel. All the efforts of Russia and her satellites, the Arabs and their friends in the Third World, failed to have Israel branded as an aggressor. For the inflammatory speeches in which Arab politicians had proclaimed the annihilation of Israel in 'total war' were still ringing in most ears throughout the world.

The war had been won; now it was a question of winning the peace. Israel made it plain to friend and foe alike that she intended to hold in pledge the conquered territories until the Arabs were prepared to accept a *modus vivendi* which, unlike the settlement after 1956, could not be jeopardized by unilateral action. At the same time the Israel government sought to solve the refugee problem. In the Gaza Strip and in the areas west of Jordan, Israel administers most of those Palestinian refugees whom Arab resistance had condemned to a wretched camp-life for nearly twenty years. Constructive resettlement has begun to look as though it may really be possible.

At the end of her second decade as an independent state, Israel's position is stronger than before. Not only has she averted the deadliest peril she has known in the course of her short history, but her military success has virtually recreated the political scene in the Near East, and thereby made it possible to look for peace on a new footing.

After a history of three thousand years, during two thirds of which a hostile world was bent on their moral and physical destruction, the Jewish people's vitality remains unimpaired. But what they need, and what with every fibre they long for, is peace, that the promise of the prophet may be fulfilled:

> ... Thus saith the Lord God; Behold I will take the children of Israel from among the heathen, whither they be gone, and will gather them on every side, and bring them into their own land; And I will make them one nation in the land upon the mountains of Israel....
> (EZEKIEL 37, 21–22)

CHRONOLOGY

B.C.

20th century	Beginning of the age of the patriarchs Abraham, Isaac and Jacob
c. 1550–1200	Canaan under Egyptian rule
14th century	Joseph and his brothers in Egypt
c. 1378–1362	Amarna age
c. 1300–1250	Servitude of the children of Israel in Egypt under Ramses II
c. 1250–1200	Exodus of Israelite tribes from Egypt under Moses. Jahve's revelation on Sinai. Start of the conquest of Canaan
c. 1220	First mention of Israel as a people on a stele of Merenptah
c. 1200	Philistines penetrate into the coastal zone of Canaan
c. 1200–1020	Age of the Judges
c. 1100–1050	First battles against the Philistines.
c. 1020–922	The united kingdom under Saul, David and Solomon
c. 1000–450	Age of the Prophets
c. 950	Solomon builds the first Temple in Jerusalem
922	Division of the kingdom
922–721	The divided kingdom — separate states of Israel and Judah
841	Jehu pays tribute to Shalmaneser III of Assyria
732	Tiglath-pileser III of Assyria conquers Damascus and the northern provinces of Israel
721	Sargon II of Assyria captures Samaria; end of northern kingdom of Israel
621	King Josiah of Juda's religious reform
609–605	Egyptian supremacy in Canaan
605	Annexation of Syria and Palestine by Nebuchadnezzar II of Babylon
587	Jerusalem destroyed by Nebuchadnezzar II; end of the southern kingdom of Judah
587–538	Babylonian exile
539	Conquest of Babylon by Cyrus II of Persia. Cyrus allows the Jews to return
538	Cyrus decrees the rebuilding of the Temple in Jerusalem
515	Consecration of the second Temple
c. 450–300	Reorganization of the economic, social and religious life in Judah by Ezra and Nehemiah
332	Alexander the Great conquers Tyre; Palestine part of the Alexandrian empire. Beginning of the Hellenistic age
c. 330–200	Palestine under Ptolemaic overlordship. Alexandria becomes a centre of Jewish life
c. 200	The Old Testament translated into Greek (Septuagint) in Alexandria
198	Beginning of Seleucid rule in Palestine
168	Antiochus IV suppresses the Jewish faith
166	Beginning of Hasmonean rising under Judas Maccabaeus
164	Rededication of the Temple in Jerusalem
140	Beginning of Hasmonean dynasty with Simon
63	End of Seleucid monarchy. Capture of Jerusalem by Pompey; Palestine under Roman rule
37–4	Herod I King of Judea. Third Temple built

A.D.

c. 7	Birth of Jesus
c. 33	Jesus crucified
c. 34	Beginning of the apostle Paul's activity
66–70	The Jewish War
70	Titus destroys Jerusalem and the Temple; end of Jewish political independence
after 70	Creation of the Jamnian Patriarchate

115–117	Revolt of the Jews of Cyrene, Alexandria, Cyprus and Mesopotamia against the Romans
132–135	Second Jewish rising against Rome under Simeon Bar-Cochba
135	Judea almost depopulated. Jerusalem rebuilt after its destruction as the Roman colony Aelia Capitolina
after 135	Patriarchal See moved to Sepphoris in Galilee
c. 138	Mitigation of Hadrian's anti-Jewish laws under his successor, Antoninus Pius, but conversion to Judaism banned
c. 100–200	Exilarch as leader of Jewry in Mesopotamia
c. 200	Activity of Jehudah ha-Nassi, completion of Mishnah in Sepphoris
224–651	Kingdom of the Sassanids. Exilarch with See at Machuza recognized as Jewish leader. The Babylonian Talmud produced by the academies of Nehardea, Sura, Machuza and Pumbeditha
313–312	Constantine the Great's Edict of Tolerance. The rise of Christianity in the Byzantine Empire leads to the ostracism and disenfranchisement of Jews in the East Roman Empire and in Europe
c. 400	Jerusalem (Palestinian) Talmud completed
425	Theodosius II suspends the Galilean Patriarchate
c. 500	Completion of Babylonian Talmud
610–632	Mohammed's activity. Rise of Islam
651	End of Sassanid dynasty, Mesopotamia becomes Arabian, caliphs recognize the Exilarchate
c. 600–1000	The heads (Geonim) of the academies of Sura and Pumbeditha are the highest spiritual authority in all Jewry
711	Spain under the Arabs; considerable Jewish immigration
c. 750	Upper castes and major part of the people of the Khazar kingdom are converted to Judaism
c. 700–800	Secession of the Karaites from rabbinical Judaism. Activity of Saadiah ben Yussuf
c. 900–1000	Flowering of Jewry in Islamic Spain
c. 1000	Migration of Jews from Mesopotamia to the West
1096	Beginning of first Crusade. Persecution of Jews in France and Germany
1099	Jerusalem falls to the Crusaders; end of Jewish community in Jerusalem
c. 1000–1100	Flowering of Jewry in Christian Spain. Activity of Jehudah ha-Levi
1179	Third Lateran Council: Christians forbidden usury. Thereafter money-lending almost entirely in Jewish hands. Anti-Jewish laws of early Christian era re-enacted
c. 1165–1204	Activity of Maimonides
1215	Fourth Lateran Council: Jews excluded from all Christian professions. Compulsory wearing of badge and hat
c. 1200–1300	Dominicans destroy Jewish religious literature
1258	Conquest of Baghdad by Mongols. End of Exilarchate
1264	A charter of Boleslaus the Pious accords Jews in Poland protection and freedom
1348–49	Plague in western and central Europe. Severe Jewish persecution in Germany. Emigration to Poland
1354	Casimir the Great increases Jewish privileges
1391	Persecution of Jews in Spain. Compulsory conversions, rise of the *marranos*
1394	Jews finally expelled from France by Charles VI
1480	Inquisition set up in Spain, directed especially at the *marranos*
1492	Jews expelled from Spain by Ferdinand and Isabella. They took refuge mainly in the Levant
c. 1550	Flowering of Jewish mysticism (Kabbalah) at Safed. Activity of Isaac Luria (Ari)
1551	Jewish communities in Poland granted self-government by a decree of Sigismund Augustus. Creation of a Jewish Diet (Waad)
1648/49	Cossack rising under Chmielnicki, mass murders of Jews and Poles
1656	Cromwell allows Jews to enter England
c. 1650–1700	Secret emigration of *marranos* from Spain and Portugal; creation of Jewish communities in West-European ports
c. 1650	Activity of Spinoza in Amsterdam
up to 1676	Sabbatai Zewi active in Turkey
c. 1750	Rabbi Israel ben Eliezer (Baal Shem Tov) active in Podola; rise of Hasidism
1768	Rising of Haidamaks in Ukraine. Severe persecution of Jews
1776	United States Declaration of Independence: 'All men have the right to practise the religion of their choice . . .'
c. 1780	Moses Mendelssohn active in Berlin. Beginning of the Jewish enlightenment, Haskalah
1789	French Revolution: declaration of human and civic rights on the North American pattern. Beginning of the emancipation of the Jewish people throughout Europe
1791	Equal citizenship conceded to Jews in France
1793/95	Second and third partition of Poland. The major part of the Jewish population of Poland under Russian rule. A 'settlement area' set up for Jews in Russia
1796	Equal rights for Jews in Holland
1806	Napoleon I founds the Jewish Sanhedrin for France

c. 1800–1850	Creation of *Wissenschaft vom Judentum*	1917	Balfour Declaration	1956	Israeli Sinai Campaign against the Egyptians
1825–55	Under Nicholas I, severe oppression of Jews in Russia	1917–20	Civil war in Russia. Mass murder of Jews in the Ukraine by White Army soldiers	1967	The 'Six-Day War' of Israel against the Arab states of Egypt, Syria, Iraq, Jordan, Saudi Arabia and the Lebanon

c. 1800–1850 Creation of *Wissenschaft vom Judentum*

1825–55 Under Nicholas I, severe oppression of Jews in Russia

1847 Equality for Jews in Prussia

1855–81 Mitigation of anti-Jewish laws in Russia under Alexander II

1860 Founding of *Alliance Israélite Universelle* by Adolphe Crémieux

1867 Equality for Jews in Austria and Hungary

1869/71 Equality for Jews throughout Germany

1870 Work of Jewish settlement starts in Palestine

1870 Equality for Jews in Italy

1871 Equality for Jews in England

1871 Founding of Anglo-Jewish Association

1874 Equality for Jews in Switzerland

c. 1880 Appearance of racial anti-Semitism in Germany

1881 Start of Jewish pogroms in Russia, 'first Aliyah' (immigration) into Palestine

1882 'May Laws' in Russia. Start of mass emigration of Jews from east to west, especially to the United States

1884 Beginning of Zionist movement in Russia (Hoveve Zion)

1894 Dreyfus affair in France

1897 First Zionist Congress in Basle under Theodor Herzl, Basle Programme

1901 Founding of Jewish National Fund by Chaim Weizmann

1901 Founding of *Hilfsverein der deutschen Juden*

1904–14 'Second Aliyah' from Russia to Palestine

1909 Tel Aviv founded

1914 Founding of American Jewish Joint Distribution Committee

1917 Russian Revolution. Equality for Jews in Russia

1917/18 Collapse of Turkish defence positions on Palestine front before the advance of British troops

1917 Balfour Declaration

1917–20 Civil war in Russia. Mass murder of Jews in the Ukraine by White Army soldiers

1919/20 Treaty of Versailles: treaties for the protection of minorities in favour of the Jews concluded with the 'border states', Poland, Lithuania, Latvia, Estonia, and the 'succession states', Czechoslovakia, Hungary, Yugoslavia and with Rumania

1920 Beginning of 'Third Aliyah' to Palestine

1920 Great Britain given Palestine Mandate

1929 Founding of Jewish Agency for Palestine

1933 Hitler becomes chancellor. Beginning of disenfranchisement of German Jews and of Jewish emigration. Concentration camps set up

1935 Nuremberg Laws

1938 'Crystal Night' 9/10 November

1939 British White Paper on Palestine

1939 Outbreak of Second World War. Complete disenfranchisement of Polish Jews. Pogroms

1940/41 Ghettos set up in Poland. Complete disenfranchisement of Jews in German-occupied countries

1941–44 Hitler's 'final solution to the Jewish question' brought about the murder of between four and five million European Jews by 'task forces' in the Soviet Union and in the extermination camps in Poland

1945 Mass extermination of Jews in German concentration camps

1947 The United Nations decide on the partition of Palestine and the foundation of the Jewish State

1948 Founding of the State of Israel — its first president Chaim Weizmann, and first Prime Minister David Ben Gurion. Jerusalem became the capital

1948/49 Jewish-Arab War (War of Liberation)

1956 Israeli Sinai Campaign against the Egyptians

1967 The 'Six-Day War' of Israel against the Arab states of Egypt, Syria, Iraq, Jordan, Saudi Arabia and the Lebanon

INDEX

ACKNOWLEDGMENTS

The authors wish to thank the many institutions and individuals both at home and abroad who have helped to produce this book, and especially the Hebrew University in Jerusalem, the Israel Museum in Jerusalem, Madame Monique Picard, Dr Willy Guggenheim and Mr Len Shirman.
Reproduction of Marc Chagall's *Jew with Torah*, by kind permission of the Galerie Rosengart, Lucerne; reproduction of Holbein's *Rehoboam* by permission of the Öffentliche Kunstsammlung, Basle.

Quotations in the text have been taken from the following editions:
Frank, A. *The Diary of a Young Girl*. Constellation Books, London, 1952.
ibn Gabirol, S. *The Improvement of Moral Qualities*. Columbia University Oriental Studies, Volume 1, New York, 1901.
Gardiner, A. H. *Egypt of the Pharaohs*. Clarendon Press, Oxford, 1961.
von Hofmannsthal, H. *The Fool and Death*. Colorado College Publications Studies Series No. 5, Colorado Springs, 1930.
ha-Levi, J. *Selected Poems*. Jewish Publication Society of America, Philadelphia, 1924.
Madariaga, S. de. *Christopher Columbus*. Hodder and Stoughton, London, 1939.
Rathenau, W. *In Days to Come*. George Allen and Unwin, London, 1921.

SOURCES OF THE ILLUSTRATIONS

The photographs for the colour plates were specially taken for this book by Hed Wimmer. All other plates not acknowledged below come from the archives of Bucher Publishers, Lucerne, or the authors. Alinari, Florence, 66, 82; Bibliothèque Nationale, Paris, 102; Foto Marburg, 14, 26, 27, 83, 110; British Museum, 15, 30, 54, 56, 61; Maximilien Bruggmann, 108; Walter P. Brunner, 152; René Burri/Magnum, 106/107; Collection Roger Viollet, Paris, 64, 67, 105, 113; Cosmopress, Geneva, 6, 135; Gewerbemuseum, Cologne, 41; Grollenberg, *Bildatlas zur Bibel*, Elsevier, Amsterdam, 14, 22, 38; Philip Halsman, 142; Hebrew University, Jerusalem, 90, 103, 111, 115, 133, 145, 148; Historia Photo, Bad Sachsa, 62, 110, 114, 136; Monique Jacot, 154; Louvre, Paris, 51; Mansell Collection, London, 104; Öffentliche Kunstsammlung, Basle, 53; W. Speiser, 144; Staatsbibliothek, Berlin, 109, 114, 122, 134; Süddeutscher Verlag, Munich, 143; Horst Tappe, 153; University of Chicago, 29; Hed Wimmer, 102.